The Intuitive Marketer

Timeless marketing principles to create and build
successful businesses

Pat Grosse

PROLOGUE

Recently, my daughters were reminiscing about using the internet when they were children. My youngest daughter was born a digital native, with access to technology for as long as she can remember. She was surprised that my eldest daughter could remember a time before technology became part of everyday life. Only eight years separate the pair of them.

I am an everyday person with a story to tell; a person who you would pass every day on the street. My story stands alongside the development of the Information Society, the dot com revolution, and the world of information overload that we live in today. The same story that runs parallel to changes in how businesses promote their products and services and interact with their customers. The most significant shifts have happened over recent years. We can't look back even five years without feeling the enormity of the way information technology has changed the face of marketing. Online shops, automated product funnels, processes to nurture prospects from social media, webinars, and video marketing. We are in danger of information overload about the choices available to turn our businesses into profit making success stories. What we need is to take a step back and evaluate these new tools and strategies with respect to our experiences and their role alongside more traditional marketing tools. Then we can make informed choices.

My journey started when door-to-door salesmen pounded the streets, computers filled entire rooms, and paper advertising was still king. Online tools are not new ideas, they are simply just tools designed to shorten the marketing journey to sales. Writing this book was an intuitive journey. It showed me how most of the advice given today is grounded in age-old marketing principles.

Contents

INTRODUCTION

The story of the Intuitive Marketer started in 2013 when, like more than 60% of business start-ups, my business showed signs of decline by the three-year mark. It certainly wasn't growing. At the same time, it was the at the very nexus when social media was beginning to make a dramatic impact on the marketing environment. Marketing models I had previously used, were no longer as successful as they had been. Over the next couple of years, websites would become necessary marketing platforms and would be required to become responsive to stay relevant for the growth of mobile phone technology. The online environment had become crowded, quickly reaching saturation point. It was a point of change.

For the next three years, I set about upgrading my marketing skills and knowledge. I joined networks, read books, attended countless webinars and workshops, even joined a couple of business Mastermind groups. Each step in this process intuitively flowed from the previous experience. Along the way, I could see why so many other businesses were also failing. In many cases, they either didn't expand or focus their marketing channels, or they were hastily adopting online platforms without understanding how they work for business purposes, losing money and confidence in the process.

Today, information technology plays a significant role in marketing. Recently, I was working with a client on a proposal involving the Internet of Things. It is predicted that 40% of jobs as we know them will disappear in the next 15 years because of next level technology. Technology-based hackathon events are now springing up to investigate ways to speed up efficiency, enhance productivity and make life easier.

I am at an age that remembers the evolution of information technology and software that helped revolutionise marketing. We take Microsoft Office for granted, but its introduction meant that we could now desktop publish in-house and the days of badly-written overhead slides were numbered. I worked in what would become a market leader, that also embraced and promoted information technology. This was at the time of the creation of the self-fulfilling vision of the Information Super Highway by such men as Al Gore and Jacques Delors. My journey as an intuitive marketer ran alongside its growing impact. I appreciate the value of technology on marketing, but haven't lost sight of its role in generating tools that bring about efficiency in the marketing process. There are online marketing gurus who claim that offline marketing is dead. Marketing is multi-platform. If they were to spend some time in the offline marketing environment, they would be amazed.

In this book, I will reveal how some of the marketing features we take for granted today evolved as information technology became embedded in our psyche. Much of the earlier technology has since given way to even more enhancements, a timely reminder that what we consider cutting-edge today will quickly become out-dated. Time doesn't stand still, but marketing principles stand the test of time; even more reason to remember that the online programs we use are simply tools that will become obsolete. Marketing is more than using online programs to generate customers and profits.

Without doubt, it's important for businesses, particularly start-ups, to understand how online programs and automation software and can be applied to help them achieve their marketing goals and to choose the marketing channels that best suit them. It's equally important to learn and apply marketing principles irrespective of technology.

With the wisdom of hindsight, I have put together a checklist of marketing priorities I would put in place as a new start-up; the first being to start with a plan from day one. If you are considering starting a business for the first time, use this checklist as a guide to focus your marketing approach.

This book is based on real-life experience. It aims to introduce some wisdom in a climate of information overload. Each of the twenty Marketing Principle includes a checklist of actions to explore and guide the reader.

Today, when I work with a client, my intuition plays a major part in identifying and targeting the critical aspects of marketing they need to focus on. The problem may not be necessarily the most obvious issue the client comes up with. I have designed a Marketing Focus Matrix that encompasses the Marketing Principles as a visual representation of the components of a long-term focus on marketing for business owners that don't have access to large marketing teams.

Here's to your success.

CHAPTER 1

THE INFORMATION VORTEX

"We are drowning in information, while starving for wisdom" - E O Wilson

The recipe for a modern-day marketing strategy:
- ☐ Develop your marketing goals
- ☐ Focus on one key strategy to change the way you market your business forever
- ☐ Find and target the right customers for your business
- ☐ Use your unique selling proposition to stand out from the crowd in a sea of sameness / crowded marketplace
- ☐ Know your figures – measure and improve your cost per acquisition
- ☐ Build your marketing funnel
- ☐ Develop your social media plan
- ☐ The money is in the list – build and segment your database
- ☐ Set up your payment gateways
- ☐ Automate your marketing processes.

Wherever you look on the internet today, there are lots of experts who are keen to teach you how to get rich if you use a combination of quick and easy steps to a killer marketing strategy. Most of these steps require mastery of an online environment that gets more complex with the introduction of even more new apps to make our lives easier. We are being bombarded with so much information that we either feel a failure if we don't implement everything we are told to do in the way we've been told, or if we do and we don't get the desired results. A lot of advice focuses on a limited field of vision, based on using technology as the front-line tool for success. Good marketing and brand development incorporate other ways to nurture trust, repeat business and new opportunities. In a crowded marketplace, success is also built on using age old marketing principles that continue to stand the test of time.

It was only a few years ago that businesses were being encouraged to set up websites that focused on presenting information about the business. In many cases, they were little more than an online trade directory for your business. Today, websites are designed to work on desktops, tablets and mobile phones. They follow people's movements and online behaviour to target advertising, link to social media and come in forms such as online shops and blogs. Facebook has become the world's number one online marketing engine and YouTube has captured a large share of the online video market. As consumers, it seems we have no secrets. Our so called wants and needs are anticipated and suggested solutions promoted to us wherever we go online. Such is the sophistication of marketing today.

If so much change has happened in a few short years, what will the marketing landscape for businesses look like in five years' time? With all this attention on online tools, what will the offline marketing environment look like?

Marketing habits have changed greatly over the last few years. Do you remember when it was vital for a business to be listed in the Yellow Pages? Today it's a lot easier to win business without meeting your customers. Automation has replaced the need to send special offer coupons in the mail or placements in newspapers. Autoresponders (marketing automation/e-mail response systems) have made it easy to sequence personalised email messages to prospects, to guide them through a nurturing and decision-making process to keep their interest until they agree to buy from you. Now we are also being invaded by SMS messages on our mobile phones.

Coming up fast is the internet of things – where our everyday appliances can analyse our usage, discover and suggest repair options for faults, or even pre-empt our desires to make our lives even easier to enjoy. What will this mean for the next era of marketing? We are living in exciting times, but what about the accumulated wisdom that got us to this point? What experience can we use in defining a good marketing strategy today?

The media have changed, but what are the underlying marketing principles that have survived the test of time? To identify exactly what these principles are, throughout this book I visit the younger me and explore my own journey, including my brief exposure in a world leading textile company, as a young mum earning my way through a database revolution, my role in a market leader in a training market niche in Europe and my recent foray into learning about the world of modern day marketing strategies.

This book is my journey into understanding what these marketing principles are. I am fortunate to have worked for a market leader in a unique niche for ten years prior to the internet explosion that began in the 2000's. Yet, at the same time, my journey frequently crossed paths with the development of technology we take for granted today. I didn't have any formal marketing education until I made a conscious decision to go back to study to begin to make sense of why we were successful.

Fast forward to the 2010's and I found myself operating a new business in a marketing vacuum. It never occurred to me to value and apply what I already knew. I just hit the deck running. I missed a lot of opportunity and eventually my business suffered as a result. After three years in business I went into panic mode and spent the next three years soaking up as much marketing know-how as I could only to discover that I already knew the principles. I was drowning myself in information, but already had the wisdom inside of me.

Here is my story.

The Number One Mistake

Intuitive Marketer Principle 1: Build in marketing from day one. Aim for at least 20% of your available time to be engaged in marketing activities.

Intuitive Marketer Principle 2: Ensure your business model is sustainable. If not, change it immediately.

> *"A man who stops advertising to save money is like a man who stops a clock to save time"* – *Henry Ford*

Even today, Henry Ford's comment makes a lot of sense, but what happens when a man, or woman, decides to leave their job and set up their own business? They're all geared up, ready to launch their passion and technical skills on the world. Marketing might not be top of mind if they have a ready-made customer base built on the networks they made whilst in a job. Or they have contacts in an exclusive, niche market. Or they think that a loan or a grant to get their business going will magically create customers, when what they really need is a marketing plan that will generate clients and income? As a grant writer, I would get enquiries from business start-ups looking for grants when what they really needed was a marketing plan.

When I started up in business, I had a ready-made customer base within a niche market. No, I didn't rely on a loan or grant, but to fund my project management services at the start, clients were reliant on grants. I was working with not-for-profit organisations. This was at a time when grants were more readily accessible, before state and federal governments cut back on programs and funding in the areas I specialised in at the time. Thus, my business model and that of many community development and education professionals like me, was unsustainable. Over the years I have seen competitors, some who even encouraged me to take a leap of faith into setting up my own business (for which I am grateful for), have returned to the job market. I could so easily have followed suit, but there's a driving force within me that has kept me resolute, even during the hard times.

Statistics show that more than 60% of new businesses fail within three years. After three healthy and comfortable years' involvement in projects in fields as diverse as e-learning, climate change, strategic planning, aged care and training innovation, opportunities began to slow down. I had a limited client base. I knew I would be heading for trouble if I didn't do anything about it. Giving up wasn't an option. Thus, started my three-year journey into learning about marketing – again. It took me those three years to realise I already had the knowledge and the experience. Somewhere along the way I had chosen to ignore latent marketing skills. I didn't value enough what I already knew. Maybe the word isn't ignore? Perhaps it was lack of self-confidence. What would the entrepreneurial mother of four in my thirties persona say if she were to see me hungrily looking for the secrets to success? Secrets I already possessed.

I have learnt a lot over the past few years; there's probably enough information and advice out there, so readily available, to prepare all of us for an MBA ten times over. But there's only so much anyone can absorb before the message becomes repetitive, especially when there are so many people out there selling, or giving away, the same knowledge. Even the sure-fire success formulas began to sound the same.

So far, I have spoken about my experience as a start-up, but Henry Ford's quote is also true for established businesses in that we must advertise to grow our sales and make money. How successful we are will depend on our marketing skills set and our understanding of our markets. Going into business, I had parked marketing on a dusty shelf in my brain. Today, I am making a concerted effort to prioritise marketing, even when we are busy with work in the pipeline.

My fundamental problem was that I did not build in marketing from day one of my new business. Simple as that. Guess what? I'm not the only one. I was relying on my reputation and existing networks like many others. You can build a business this way, but my business model meant that I was reliant on my limited pool's access to grants to support them and to pay my business for its services. I was focusing on a small segment of the not-for-profit sector. Too small to be sustainable. I wasn't just dependent on them getting the funding, I even applied for the grant funding on their behalf. It wasn't just risky. In one case, I successfully applied for the funding and didn't get the gig.

Today, we operate in clearly defined market segments across not-for-profit organisations and clubs, as well as businesses. I have extended our grant writing services to include an online grant writing course and a mentoring program. I have created other programs and services, including products to sale as passive income. As people say, all businesses are in the business of marketing.

Let's go back to the thirty-something me.

Results – The Success Juggernaut

For your business, exchange the words in this statement with your business goals or achievements:

"What if you could *develop and promote a variety of workshops in four locations,* knowing full well that *there would be enough demand for eight*? What if you could *organise conferences on random topics* and get *participation from thirteen countries*?"

I achieved this success. I was an energetic mother of four young children, working with the support of a loving, extended family. I travelled across the UK and Europe as part of the job and went back to study for a degree at the same time. Obviously, our marketing worked, and we were busy. Does this sound familiar? We hear about these amazing women who seem to be able to juggle it all. I was one of them. I had it all worked out. I had so much energy in those days. I had inner confidence and as a mother, I also had the super woman complex.

Fast-forward to my fledgling business. I had the ingredients for success, but instead of trusting my inner self, I allowed the deafening roar of too many online marketing gurus sprouting the 'your business needs to follow my million-dollar marketing formula' to confuse and delay my mission to get my business back up and running. Fear, lack of confidence, information overload; all combined to keep me going around in circles

I heard so many conflicting nuggets of advice that it's not that difficult to get confused, or to spend thousands on a promise that doesn't work. It's amazing how many of our clients are now coming forward who have been stung by marketing experts who've taken their money and not delivered the results. They heard compelling sales pitches accompanied by a strong educational content designed to stamp the guru's authority, who then provided evidence of social proof through testimonies of clients who'd already worked with them and got results. It's not a one size fits all solution and what works for some, won't work for others no matter how good the guru's team members are. When I first speak to business owners that have been stung, at first they are quite rude and very wary. They're hurt and don't trust anybody. That is, until I pick up on the missing connection that leads to the ah-ha moment for the client.

As the owner of a struggling business, I didn't have the thousands of dollars to invest in these "get rich if you follow our lead" programs but I have heard of people who continually invested until it hurt. It is so easy to get carried away with listening to cleverly crafted sales talk that grabs you emotionally and you are compelled to buy. Luckily, I was taught the marketing sales scripts of some of the world's best sales people so that whenever I got the follow-up sales call after attending workshops, I would listen for the usual cues such as "on a scale of 1 to 10..." or "if money wasn't an issue...". I would use the opportunity to examine the caller's sales technique before explaining why I didn't have the funds (I really didn't). I would then wait for the phone to be put down at the other end soon after. I obviously wasn't the right sort of lead.

There are some excellent programs out there that do deliver on the promise, but it is important to check out with people who have already purchased these programs before you buy. You are risking thousands of dollars, so why not do your homework first?

THE INTUITIVE MARKETER

This book isn't about promises. If you want my advice, contact me directly. This book is about my discovery about fundamental marketing strategies that are important irrespective of the latest online 'solving all your problems now' program. Technology and software has its place, but as I will explain later, it is merely a tool, not the one-stop marketing solution. Success comes once you understand this and promote your products and services from this mindset.

This book is about how I was an 'intuitive' marketer, how I forgot everything I knew, and my journey back. It's for you if you are overwhelmed by all the marketing advice out there and want proof of timeless strategies so that you can apply techniques that will kick start your business marketing engine.

Fundamentally, we are in the business of marketing; if we don't market, we quickly have no business. Some would take this further and say we are in show business; an interesting thought. Starting with the principle of building marketing into your activities from the very first day, I will explain how I rediscovered 20 principles, most of which the younger me knew and the older me forgot.

The first of these principles, integral to all business is to build in marketing from day one. It is so easy to forget this principle, especially in the good times when work and income is flowing inwards. If you don't, the flow will slow down and stop. Start with your existing clients who can easily assist you by giving you feedback on why they chose you. They are also your main source of referrals, so how can you reward them? Clients can also change direction or no longer need your services, so consider how you can plan to fill the void or offer them the next solution so that they stay with you longer.

> **Intuitive Marketer Principle 1: Build in marketing from day one. Aim for at least 20% of your available time to be engaged in marketing activities.**
>
> ☐ Segment your target market and their behaviours
> ☐ Identify your busy and quiet times of year
> ☐ Structure marketing channels and campaigns to level out slow periods
> ☐ Set up pipeline for 90 days and up to 2 years
> ☐ Set SMART goals, prioritise actions and review every 90 days

Identify your target audience so that you can focus your energy and resources on getting the right message to the buyers that care and can pay. Segmenting allows you to get personal with your market by speaking the language of the prospective buyer. If you can identify the busy and quiet times of your year, you can build in different marketing channels and campaigns to level out the slow periods and any potential cash-flow crises Go one step further and systematically set up your marketing pipeline for at least three months and even out to over the first two years. You may need to think laterally to get results. My panic started when I looked over the 18-month horizon and saw a dry river bed. Don't let this happen to you.

We had a client who had busy and quiet times during the year. He had the online marketing environment covered. He used his website, eBay and Facebook, but because his products were seasonal, his sales were not consistent enough to sustain a steady flow of sales. There had to be an alternative market. He tried advertising in magazines, but these also attracted seasonal audiences. Working with him, we identified trade expos as a place to capture new pipeline leads and follow-up sales. All he needed was three expos across the year to ensure a steady flow of leads. Problem solved.

Intuitive Marketer Principle 2: Ensure your business model is sustainable. If not, change it immediately.

- ☐ What is the valuable proposition of the product or service you are offering?
- ☐ How does it stand out from the competition? *This becomes your unique message*
- ☐ Who are you trying to reach? Are they the right market? Can they pay? *Talk directly to your paying customers and prospects*
- ☐ What strategies are you using to reach your prospects?
- ☐ Do you have the skills in-house or are you outsourcing? *Focus your marketing tools on your lucrative customers.*
- ☐ How do you propose to get the product or service to your customers? Have you built in opportunities for value-adding and upgrading? *Build a succession of products or services.*
- ☐ What are the activities and resources required to develop and deliver the product or service? *Ensure cost of inputs and delivery are less than sale.*
- ☐ Who can help you – *partners, joint ventures etc.*
- ☐ Be clear about your revenue streams, costs of customer acquisition and cost of sales *Determine viable, profitable, fee structures*
- ☐ Identify and mitigate risks *Plan to succeed from the start*

Measures of Sustainability (time, money, and effort)

- ☐ How are you being most effective with your time? Are there parts of the process that could by improved in relation to your time? What are possible solutions?
- ☐ Are there any financial blockages or drains in the processes? How can you create the best service/outcome at the lowest cost / highest profitability?
- ☐ Are the processes consistent, efficient, and effective? How can they be improved?

THE INFORMATION VORTEX

Sometimes your business model isn't sustainable because you're pitching the wrong product or service to the wrong audience, or your audience can't afford to pay. There are business model tools available to assist with getting your model right and avoiding heartache and business failure.

One such model is the Business Model Canvas (Strategyzer). The Business Model Canvas helps you to identify your value propositions for your various customer segments, how you plan to generate interest in your products and services and how you plan to deliver them. At the back end of the operation, the Business Model Canvas guides you to identify your key activities, resources and partners – to develop and bring products and services to market. Underpinning these activities are your proposed cost structures and revenue streams.

Use a business model tool to define the right model for your business.

There is a lot of free education and information out there today about marketing available to business owners. The challenge is to reach into the information vortex, sift through the sales pitches and find the right marketing channel design and model for your business.

Later in this book I have put together a Focused Marketing Matrix that we recommend you refer to when putting together 90 day marketing plans, starting at day one.

Whatever happens, don't stop marketing, even when business is good.

CHAPTER 2

CLUELESS

"The way of success is the way of continuous pursuit of knowledge" – Napoleon Hill

Intuitive Marketer Principle 3: Use the tools of the day to evoke emotion - people respond to words, expressions and imagery

Intuitive Marketer Principle 4: Education is key to demonstrating trust and credibility

Intuitive Marketer Principle 5: Keep up to date with your marketing knowledge. Use a variety of channels which may include: books, workshops, webinars, Mastermind groups, networks, mentors and literature.

Why isn't marketing a compulsory subject at school? Seriously? It wasn't even on the curriculum when I was at school. If it were, I'd have been at the front of the class, eager to learn. Instead, in search of a non-academic discipline, I made the other smart move. I travelled across town once a week for a year to my sister's school for after school lessons in computer studies. This was in the days when we put together binary code that was sent away to one of the only two places in town which housed massive computers that could test our insignificant calculations. Our coding would be transferred onto ticker tape and put through one of these machines. It would take up to two weeks to get the results. Today it would take a couple of seconds and the push of a button. At the time, I didn't realise what a smart move I'd made and how technology would influence me through my life's journey and prepare me for the worlds of e-learning and online marketing. Was this intuition?

Even today, marketing is an elective in schools that sometimes doesn't get over the line because not enough students choose it. Yet government policy encourages entrepreneurs to set up businesses, and governments are prepared to invest in business and marketing growth, which leads to jobs, a competitive advantage and export markets. Credit should go to the enterprising schools and tertiary colleges with the foresight to help students put together, test and pitch their business ideas with marketing plans.

The thirty-something me was on the advisory committee of a local college business program and was asked to judge marketing pitches from the students. The students got practice and mentoring guidance from business owners during the course of the year. They presented their business and marketing plans and the winners got additional support to take their ideas to market. The flavour of the day was mobile phones. What do today's students choose?

With little support and preparation, it is easy for somebody to set up a business and yet be clueless about marketing. It's no wonder a billion-dollar industry has evolved around teaching businesses how to market their products and services. There are so many business owners desperate for the magic formula that they are prepared to pay tens of thousands at the drop of a hat, or should I say at the end of an extremely convincing presentation by a master in the art of selling. Success is not guaranteed and to be fair, even the most gifted mentor can't guarantee you'll make millions if you don't put in the hard work.

For the entrepreneur who wasn't taught marketing at school, it's not at the top of mind when making the decision to go into business. The desire to go into business is built on technical knowledge or passion and it is tempting to build the product and service and expect people to come. We so easily turn to the internet and social media to solve our marketing dilemmas. We seek the trending marketing channel solution of the day and if it doesn't work, we move on to the next. There is no field of dreams. We are clueless.

I left school clueless. My journey from clueless to success began in my twenties, when I worked for a worldwide textile giant. It was on the cusp of the decline of the industry that was still holding onto the last vestiges of opulence and bygone success. Our induction information included a booklet of the companies within the group – and they included some of the most iconic business names of the time. It was the 1980s, and the most popular marketing channels we operated with were trade and women's magazines, international knitting weeks, trade shows, face-to-face visits, networks and selling over the phone.

Working in the sales department, I had the extra responsibility of managing a fibre sample room. One day, I was asked to work with a regional salesman to come up with names for a new colour range. I did not have a clue. The salesman did. He was evoking powerful images based on popular European tourist resorts. The end user would be attracted to the colour and the imagery of their favourite holiday destinations. This evocation extended into the garments being modelled. Today we would call it emotional direct response marketing. I knew this incident was important to me, but at the time I didn't know why.

A good example of emotional response marketing in practice today is through well-presented social media ads. People share and respond to what they identify with, usually the solution to a problem or something that brings them joy (pain or pleasure). In an era when a website owner must capture the visitor within seven seconds, the written copy and imagery are paramount. Who can resist cuddly puppies? What about those killer headlines? The young me, in my early days of employment, learnt the power of words and imagery, but it took some time to make the connection with today's social media and website copywriting. The experience with the shade card, though insignificant, stayed with me. My intuition was at play.

Intuitive Marketer Principle 3: Use the tools of the day to evoke emotion - people respond to words, expressions and imagery.

- ☐ Speak directly to the one person – the ideal client (imagine them, their name, what they do, where they hang out etc.)
- ☐ Become them – their fears, frustrations, dreams, needs and wants
- ☐ Find out what motivates them
- ☐ Speak in their language
- ☐ Choose your imagery to get your message across visually

It was in my thirties that I set out to make up for my earlier lack of knowledge of marketing. I even studied marketing as part of my degree as a mature student and then specialised with a diploma in education marketing. The purpose? To formalise what I was intuitively doing in my job. Studying for qualifications gave me some good insights which I still apply today, but they were academic in nature and didn't include the basic principles I learnt on my journey. I had these worked out without knowing why they worked. It would take the future me to figure it out.

"When the student is ready, the teacher will appear" - Zen Proverb

Fast forward to four years ago and here I was, three years into the business and desperate to update my marketing skills. They say that when the student is ready, the teacher will appear. For me that was a procession of 'teachers' and I bet most of them don't even know the impact they had on me. If the way of success is the way of continuous pursuit of knowledge (Napoleon Hill), my journey became a combination of workshops, networks, business Mastermind groups, webinars and Mr Kindle. Here's how it has played out to date.

Marketing Club Membership

Early in my business, before I employed an assistant, I outsourced work to a virtual assistant. It turned out she ran a local chapter of a business entrepreneurs' marketing network. She invited me to a meeting where the network gurus presented a marketing seminar I needed to hear at that moment in time. So, of course I joined their inner circle. I paid my monthly fee and in exchange got to monthly meetings and professional development workshops, as well as listened avidly to the regular CDs I was sent each month by snail mail as part of my membership package. I was the hungry client. I would probably still be a member today had it not been for their ambition in introducing new membership levels whilst reducing the benefits to my membership level, and the subsequent break-up of the gurus' partnership. This entrepreneurs' network was exactly what I needed to spark my journey at that time. The two ex-partners still operate independently today and I occasionally listen to their webinars. One focuses on sales and the other on marketing. Joining a marketing network helps focus and also access to experts and mentors, especially if you can't afford a mentor on your own. I still value their CDs today and listen to them occasionally in the car.

Webinars

Step two of my enlightened journey came about as part of a two-day professional development event organised by the entrepreneurs' marketing network. It was the first time I had been exposed to blatant selling from the stage. It was like this. Deliver a couple of high profile keynote presentations that educate the hungry attendees just enough to whet their appetite and to prepare them for a stream of presentations from prominent Australian entrepreneurial marketing experts. Each expert would deliver enough educational content to get prospects excited enough to buy into their two to twenty thousand-dollar packages with prices discounted as a favour to the organisers, but only for the next "fifteen minutes" or the next "three or four people" with an added bonus. They would plant seeds about their irresistible packages throughout the presentation, starting with a taster at the beginning, followed by stories of success and testimonials throughout the presentation. Bring on the "must buy now or I miss out" panic button. Seriously though, the key is educational content. This was invariably second to none when it came to raising the trust of the audience that these people were the real deal. It had to be good because otherwise nobody would buy the product packages. I bought a webinar program package.

The irony of the situation was that I had been running webinars for years in education. I had even organised them for a national peak body for adult education. What drove me to opt for the webinar package I don't know. Maybe it was intuition because I cannot, and will not, complain. I got more value than I would have ever imagined. Yes, the package was about training entrepreneurs to make money from webinars, but the value-add benefits were so totally unexpected and I am still reaping the rewards today.

Training people to become webinar experts means that they get the chance to practice live to the webinar guru's list comprising both students and non-students. My learning went through the roof because of the knowledge of other webinar students who were experts in their fields, again for free. Webinars are the ideal, time saving, way to get professional development without leaving home or the office. It's also possible to register and if you miss the session, get a recording, although I have noticed some short-sighted webinar presenters have ceased this practice. I became a webinar junkie. I would attend webinars at any time of day or night, even those delivered from overseas. As my knowledge grew, so did my appetite for innovation and that's where overseas webinars come in. Learning is global.

I have listened into so many webinars over the years that I've heard just about all the major Australian internet experts. That leaves the lesser known marketers who are also repeating the same messages to saturation point. I now reach out to learning from overseas marketing gurus who have different messages and appear to be constantly pushing the envelope in terms of innovation. As with the workshops, the quality webinars are those that educate. I am more inclined to buy into programs if I have received some new process or knowledge that benefits what I do and how I do it. Unfortunately, there are still marketers out there who can't master the delivery of a webinar.

Recently I turned off a webinar presentation from one of Australia's leading Facebook marketers who spent too much time promoting their Mastermind program and did not provide enough education content. Was he selling his high value programs based on his reputation because he certainly didn't convince me of his skills on his webinar? Another well respected marketing guru recently spent the whole of his webinar promoting his workshop. I've attended one of his workshops, which he spent promoting his high-level package. As long as there are people like this, the webinar guru will continue to be in demand for people who seriously want to be successful.

Intuitive Marketer Principle 4: Education is key to demonstrating trust and credibility

☐ Develop a plan of what you want to learn and allow the world of learning to open up in the most amazing ways.

Authors/Speakers Network

Webinars can be grouped together as summits: groups of webinars held over a few days, a week or more. Through one of these summits, I was introduced to the next person to influence my journey. This expert was for authors. I'm still on that journey and she is someone I respect as an expert in this field. Her summit was promoted by the webinar expert whose package I'd bought into. I listened in to the summit presentations and bought the set of recordings as a I didn't have the opportunity to listen to them all at the time. Not long after the summit, she partnered with an internet marketer to set up a speakers' network and to train authors in marketing skills. The internet marketer has worked behind the scenes with some of the most prominent marketing gurus in the world and is a silent gem in the industry. Between the two of them, they introduced me to marketing principles and advanced practical techniques that I continue to use with my clients today. I apply their variation of the four P's of marketing that makes a lot of sense for my clients. The value of this education has been far more than that provided by anybody else. It is unfortunate that this business partnership is also no longer together.

Both the webinar package and the speakers program included opportunities to attend face-to-face workshops. Again, it was the webinar package that led me to another guru who would influence my journey in just three days. He is a New York Times bestselling author. In this case, he condensed everything I needed to know at the time about internet marketing into these three days. Yes, three full days that started promptly at nine a.m. and finished just after six p.m. each day. They were packed full of content and the investment was my time, meals and accommodation. The educational content was free. I have since attended similar workshops for one or two-days duration, all educational, but none as intense as this. Yes, there were the offers during the three days, and no, I wasn't in a position to take them up or I already had the skills and knowledge they were trying to sell. This marketing expert is based in the UK and I listen in to his webinars when I get the chance.

Mastermind

Referring back to the entrepreneurs' marketing network, their membership package aimed to nurture members to enrol in their Mastermind program. At the time, I had probably been in a position to invest in the Mastermind program, but my intuition prevented me from taking the step. It turned out my instinct was correct. There were mixed responses from people who joined this Mastermind program. Some found it useful, others did not. Instead, another member of the network approached three of us to suggest we create our own Mastermind group. A Mastermind program is where two or more people come together to discuss their businesses openly and with trust. The premise is that there is an additional entity in the room bigger than the members combined; the Mastermind.

Four of us met for a one-day workshop, and three of us continued for three more years. We would meet by phone for two hours every Monday night and face-to-face for a whole day once every three months. We used the same reading room in an old priory for every meeting. When we walked into the room, we could sense the extra presence that was the Mastermind. It was a wonderful opportunity to discuss our businesses and leave with a plan for the next 90 days. We would also share books, readings and professional development learnings. We were focussed. However, like all good things, our Mastermind group ran its course. I look back on it as a vital element in my pursuit of knowledge.

If you can get together two or three business owners who can commit to weekly calls and quarterly face-to-face meetings, consider Napoleon Hill's definition of the Mastermind (Think and Grow Rich) and use it well.

Mentoring

I am a mentor. I have been both an informal mentor and provide mentoring as a business service. My clients achieve success and win awards. So why can't I find the right mentor for my needs?

Despite this, one recommendation I would give is to find a mentor who can help you to focus so that you get to where you want to be quicker. It's a lonely journey, so find a mentor who will guide you and keep you focused. You may need a succession of mentors on your journey, satisfying different needs. There are a lot of mentors out there, but it is important to get the right one for you. I had two attempts at finding a mentor and neither were right for my needs at the time. This is my one regret.

I currently have an informal mentor who is not a marketing expert, but who nevertheless, guides me well.

Business Networks

I can remember sitting at my desk, a couple of years into my business, chatting to a business acquaintance on Skype. It was like she was in the next room. When you're a solopreneur, which I was at the time, it can get quite lonely. Skype took away some of this sense of loneliness by providing the illusion of the colleague next door. She commented in a women's business network meeting that she used to organise before moving to the Northern Territory, on how having somebody available to talk to, even if we chose not to chat, helped to dispel the sense of solitude.

Living in regional Australia, it is difficult to find business networks to join outside of the local chambers of commerce, so I joined a business network that meets monthly for the day in Melbourne. For me this involves a commitment of six hours travel each day (three hours each way). Despite this commitment, this has proven beneficial because of the sense of community and referrals that go on between the 140 plus members. Through this network it is easy to identify experts for whatever services we need. Even online, we recognise each other in Facebook groups. A word of warning. Don't expect immediate results. It can take months to get a flow of connections. Networking works best when you allow time to create and nurture relationships.

There are many networks to choose from, mainly in large metropolitan areas and I wonder, if I lived in Melbourne, would I be constantly spending my time networking? I recently spoke to a colleague at a network meeting who admitted that she spent so much time networking that she couldn't see the wood from the trees. There but for the grace of God go I.

Be selective about which networks you join. Get to know the other members of the network. Stand in your authority. The best network I belong to has a sense of community. Everyone has the opportunity to practice and present their pitch, as well as opportunities to follow-up areas of interest and promote each other's products and services outside meetings. This network works.

Books

Gathering all this knowledge is exhausting. Workshops, networking, Mastermind. What about the books? Asking for a Kindle for a birthday present was probably one of the best presents I've ever asked for and got. My Kindle is my font of all knowledge. I have been known to read some books a few times. One book discloses more knowledge every time I read it. It's like I'm reading it for the first time. Here is a summary of some of the books have I been harvesting.

At the top of the list is Napoleon Hill's "Think and Grow Rich". Whether he did or did not interview 500 business leaders after a conversation with Andrew Carnegie, the content of the book is remarkable. It's here that we are introduced to the Mastermind concept. Alongside this book is "The Science of Getting Rich" by Wallace D Wattles. This book has a focus on the creative brain over competition. I fully understand where this concept is coming from. For me, my recent journey into marketing also involved creating new products to add to my marketing funnel, but also as a way to convert my thoughts into ideas and into physical manifestations. The younger me also knew that it was wiser to create new workshop and conference ideas than to focus on what the competition was doing.

Both of these books have a focus on the Law of Attraction – the ability to attract into our lives whatever we focus on. Before I started in business, I had no idea about the Law of Attraction. It's amazing how many business owners do know about it and follow its principles; whether it's an accountant who applies it in their advice to business owners, or the tradie who 'allowed' me to come along when he needed help. Or the business acquaintance who puts her business ideas 'out there' and attracts what she wants. It's like a philosophy that's kept secret from the world at large.

Another life-changing book for me was "The Cashflow Quadrant" by Robert Kiyosaki. This book helped me to review my business model. It helped me refocus aspects of my business through understanding the need to create passive income channels to help me build a business as opposed to striving to "buy myself a job". My early business model was 100% reliant on buying myself a job. This is not what I wanted. I have created self-learning programs, training manuals and resources which can be accessed online. My vision was also to build a business with employees, which is why I took on an assistant. We want to be our own boss, but do we also want to be our own employee? If you are a services business, is the income dependent on you working in the business. I recommend all new business owners read this book.

Other books in my collection include "The E-Myth Revisited" by Michael Gerber, especially his distinction between the technician, manager and entrepreneur, the how to become a millionaire "just like me" guides, motivational makeovers including Hay House classics and any number of miracle marketing formula books. I read and digested them all until my knowledge became tacit. One marketing book stands out from the rest. "Influence: The Psychology of Persuasion" by Dr Robert Cialdini. I've read it three times and every time I read it, I learn something new. I have used my knowledge of how the not-for-profit sector works to develop marketing programs for positioning them in front of their audiences based on my learnings from this book alone. To me, it totally makes sense.

I am now at saturation point.

> **Intuitive Marketer Principle 5: Keep up to date with your marketing knowledge. Use a variety of channels which may include: books, workshops, webinars, Mastermind groups, networks, mentors and literature.**
>
> **Possible avenues of learning:**
> - ☐ Marketing clubs or groups
> - ☐ Business networks
> - ☐ Online networks
> - ☐ Mastermind groups
> - ☐ Webinars
> - ☐ Face-to-face workshops
> - ☐ Articles/blogs
> - ☐ Conferences
> - ☐ Books
> - ☐ Mentors

Beyond Saturation

Today, I keep my Kindle by my side. I still maintain my connection to the webinar guy and continue to read his frequent email blogs. I even attended one of his two-day workshops at the beginning of this year to refresh my knowledge. The Mastermind group has long gone, but we keep in touch. After attending workshops delivered by a couple of Australia's most prominent internet marketers, I decided that walking away with no new knowledge was a clear sign for me to stop procrastinating and put my knowledge into practice.

Yet through it all, I felt I was missing out on some vital points about marketing. Much of the focus is on how to get rich online. Surely this is a two-dimensional viewpoint? What about the other stuff? The stuff that the younger me did? Marketing principles I am exploring in this book?

Let me give you an example of a basic customer engagement tool that, surprisingly, some notable entrepreneurs miss when they run events.

Food for Thought

How many times have you been to events and it's been up to you to find your own food and drink? If this has never happened to you, then you are lucky. This concept was totally alien to me the first time I came across it. The younger me, who worked in the European Briefing Unit, at the time a market leader in training people how to source and manage project funding from the European Union, would be horrified at the lack of attention to food. Food was an important factor in the quality of the workshops we organised. Never mind the program, the food was just as important. The menu for every meal was scrutinised and negotiated and we even went as far as accommodating and feeding speakers and workshop facilitators the night before each event. Looking after these people made a difference to the camaraderie of the team the next day, even if on one occasion we took a conference participant out for dinner instead of a speaker by mistake. That was embarrassing.

Have good food available for delegates and you get a happy crowd, good networking and people leave with a positive vibe. I have noticed that since I mentioned to a well networked marketing guru that they were missing out on an important part of the client nurturing process, their workshops and those of their network of expert colleagues are now providing lunch and refreshments. People are staying longer, networking and relaxing, as well as not disappearing for good at lunchtime. They are in a better frame of mind to be sold to. It doesn't cost a lot to feed people. It's widely known in the education and community development sectors about the benefits of food to engage people, so why are so many business and marketing experts so clueless?

In the same way that marketing should be incorporated into the business from day one, so should a plan and action to keep up to date with emerging (online) marketing tools. Many of the online experts were early adopters of Facebook, LinkedIn, CRM database systems, YouTube and whatever comes next. I was an early adopter of email, the World Wide Web, Microsoft Office, webinars and other tools we now take for granted. I lost ground when I took my eye off the ball with the emergence of social media. The key is that these are simply tools to assist with marketing. They effectively facilitate parts of the customer acquisition, nurturing and sales process. There is so much information about how to use these tools, but what about the principles behind the tools? How do the tools fit within an effective marketing strategy? One with depth that also includes the physical and visual aspects that contribute to a brand, positioning within the marketplace, innovation and product life-cycles? A marketing strategy that also allows for the continual acquisition of marketing knowledge and skills? Adding depth to marketing contributes to standing out from the crowd.

Even if you start out clueless about marketing, trust your intuition and let life take you on an amazing journey of discovery and learning. When the time is right, the teacher will appear, especially in the age of technology. Go with the flow.

CHAPTER 3

FREEFALL

*"Life may throw curve balls, but when it throws
the dream ball, take aim, hit for six and celebrate"*
- Pat Grosse

Intuitive Marketer Principle 6: To be the market leader in your niche, surround yourself with the right experts and networks and be prepared to take risks

Intuitive Marketer Principle 7: Know your niche and be consistent

I fell into marketing. Really. By accident, I literally fell into a job people would fight for. I fell into a job that would take me around the UK and to Brussels on a regular basis. I got to witness the machinations of European politics at a time when Margaret Thatcher resigned, the Single European Market and the European Union came into being, and crises such as mad cow disease as well as the expansion from twelve to fifteen-member states. I started employment in the European Briefing Unit at the University of Bradford, the week that Eastern Germany opened up the Berlin Wall to the West in 1989, signalling the start of Re-Unification of Germany in 1990. What a fanfare for change.

My journey into the role was unplanned and started out through an accident. Rescuing my then thirteen-month old daughter from eating worms in the garden, I picked her up and subsequently slid outside the back door. A mother's instinct led to me falling awkward, breaking my ankle, to protect her. The break came after I'd applied for two jobs at a time when I wasn't sure whether I wanted to return to work. I was following my intuition. As luck would have it, I scored interviews with both employers. The first employer just accepted my reason for withdrawal from the interview. The second, the local university, opted to interview me at home. The immediate job wouldn't wait, but I was offered a mobile secretarial position once I was able to walk. Six weeks later, still on crutches, I found myself in the personnel office, luckily one level (two flights of stairs) up, just as the fire alarm went off and hundreds of students were making their way down to the ground floor at the same time.

My third assignment was with the European Briefing Unit, a research unit of the Department of European Studies, which had received seed funding to provide services for businesses to prepare for the Single European Market in three years' time. It was a twenty hour a week secretarial role to begin with. Nobody had any idea of the amazing journey we would experience over the next ten years.

The Unit had been operating a year before I came along; still in its infancy. It was set up with three years' seed funding and lasted for twenty years, closing down when the European Briefing Officer, the founding staff member and also the Head of the Unit, retired.

Know Your Market

To be successful, we broke conventions. The first rule we broke was to "know your market". Our market was meant to be small and medium-sized businesses, but we were never able to align with that market. The European Briefing Officer had outstanding political understanding as she had been a European Young Liberal earlier in life, as well as being an incredibly knowledgeable academic. Only today do I appreciate that our supposed market would have taken us on an equally amazing journey had we had one iota of understanding about what made them tick. The Single European Market did have some potential benefits for businesses and the free movement of goods, capital, people and services. The older me would have been more comfortable with this market. However, we would have had competition for relevance with local government offices that also set up advice centres to assist businesses prepare for the Single European Market. Instead, we intuitively found other sectors we were able to capture and become a market leader. These sectors were agencies seeking funding from the European Community, which later became the European Union, and that included local government, education at all levels, the voluntary and community development sectors. We niched the sectors within our workshops and conference programs. The business sector was not one of them.

The first acts of the European Briefing Unit were to publish academic publications about the Single European Market and to set up conferences. The early conferences, some before my time, were not highly successful, but we quickly identified the European Social Fund, one of Europe's largest grants for training for employment, would generate enough interest to fill our events. We had stepped out of focusing on businesses into focusing on the other sectors as a whole – further education, higher education, local government, community development and the voluntary sector. All sectors had an interest in grants and all were applying to the same funding buckets. We designed our conferences and workshops to accommodate across all sectors, and we were a success. We were able to combine policy and invite the European Commission to our events to announce the latest changes with workshop activities targeted to cover the interests of each sector.

Becoming a market leader meant that we did have competition. However, the competition just wasn't us. People could copy our approach, but we had a good enough reputation that most of our conferences and major workshops involved participation from one of the European institutions and other policy making organisations. Our groups got briefings at the European Parliament in Strasbourg and

Brussels, the European Commission, the European Court of Justice and the European Bank for Reconstruction and Development. On occasions, we also took groups to NATO. This was also reflected in our study visits to Brussels, where our itineraries were littered with presentations, mostly at the institutions themselves. It was only when our workshop participants told us that they'd tried something similar and had found it very difficult to get speakers that I appreciated the success of our reputation.

Timing

Our success wasn't purely luck or accidental. We used our intuition and took risks. Big ones. We were prepared to stand out from the competition. In 1994 the European Union introduced a new five-year framework for the European Social Fund. It was a major change that took an extended time in developing and approving. Like our competitors, we monitored the evolution of the policy documents and when the predictions were that everything would be done and dusted by November, we opted for a March date in the following year to organise a conference on the new framework. Competitors opted for any time from November to February. We were the only ones who put our conference date out so far into the future. As each date came and went, we observed each event cancellation until it got to March and we were just about the last ones standing. Yet there was still no confirmation.

The other two staff members took a group of Taiwanese diplomats to Brussels the week before the scheduled date of the conference. I was left on my own with the support of a secretarial work-placement student and the universities' short course team who managed registrations. The Director of the Unit came to me daily for an update. We were getting inundated with registrations. People were getting desperate. This was a big event. We changed the venue to a larger lecture theatre to accommodate the influx of angry people who wouldn't entertain waiting lists. Yet we still didn't have confirmation that the European Commission speaker would be able to attend and deliver the new framework and criteria. They were hoping to, but processes were still happening right up to that point. We could have done what the others did and cancel, but we didn't.

The other staff members came back to a tense situation. The conference was due to take place on Thursday. We had organised a speaker's dinner for Wednesday evening. We had booked dinner and accommodation for the European Commission speaker as well as the UK Department of Employment speaker and the workshop leaders. Tuesday came and still no news until I got a fax, simply saying, "see you tomorrow night". We did it! We pulled it off. This conference was the first time the new funding instrument had been presented anywhere in Europe, even a day ahead of formal presentations to member states. Perfect timing. It could have been a public relations disaster. Instead, the secretarial student won a regional award.

Intuitive Marketer Principle 6: To be the market leader in your niche, surround yourself with the right experts and networks and be prepared to take risks

- ☐ Be clear about your niche and your value proposition
- ☐ Identify and connect with strategic partners and key influencers (search for them on LinkedIn)
- ☐ Join their networks
- ☐ Be confident about your proposition and use it to challenge your risk mindset

---

The Intuitive Copywriter

When you think about promotional marketing, among the first things that comes to mind are social media, e-newsletters and landing pages. The thirty-something me would have said flyers, press releases and brochures. Even though we had email, not many of our prospects did, so our major marketing channel was the postal service. There were evenings and weekends when I employed free child labour and my living room looked like a mail sorting office.

We were at the nexus between the analogue world and the digital world we take for granted today.

Even though I was technologically savvy, more about that later, there were some new software programs I didn't take to, notably desktop publishing programs such as Quark Express and Page Maker. I was never going to be the next great visual artist. Yet I did master Microsoft Word and was able to manipulate its elements to give our documents a desktop published look. The secret was simple – use a consistent format. I used colour to distinguish between events, and gloss finish paper, as simple as that. The call to action was to return the tear-off slip by mail or fax (later to include email). There were no buttons to take the visitor to an online registration. So, you can imagine how amused, I was, when somebody commented that they couldn't compete with our 'professional looking brochures and flyers.

It wasn't just the look; it was also the content that mattered. It seems I had a talent for copywriting. Although the Head of the Unit, who originally wrote the copy, was very good at 'descriptive' language (which was good for tutoring), her skills did not extend to words that sell. As our promotional literature was checked and processed through the Short Course Unit, it was more time effective for me to write the copy. This cut down the process by two weeks as fewer edits were made. Yes weeks, not days, hours or minutes that we are used to today. With the proliferation of websites and online promotional tools, it is more important than ever to have a good copywriter available. Even one-word change could make the difference between struggle and success. Social media advertising is flexible to the point that businesses can carry out A/B testing – testing multiple adverts to see which one works best. In those days, we had just one chance.

The Power of the Brand

What was the secret of our success? I would say consistency:

- We cancelled very few events, if at all.
- We had a consistent formula for the design of our workshops
- We had a consistent formula for the development of conferences in partnership with subject experts
- We paid attention to the food
- Our promotional brochures had a consistent format that people recognised
- Family ate last (and we slept in the cheaper hotel rooms in favour of our participants)
- We used practitioners who were working in the industry
- We organised speaker's dinners which led to healthy camaraderie at our events.

Basically, we created a brand.

We had a strong brand reputation. So much so that somebody once told us that when they thought of the European Union they thought of the three B's. The first was the university of Bristol that had a very strong European politics department. The second was Birmingham which was home to a major European employment initiative. Bradford, the home of the European Briefing Unit was the third. Not bad for a core staff of three.

So, what went wrong? Why, when I started my business, did I not build marketing into my planning from the onset? Yes, I put together a brochure and business cards, but they didn't look professional. I didn't create a marketing system. I was unclear about my market and what I was offering. Initially, my market was registered training organisations and adult education centres that already knew me. However, this was a small, ever decreasing market because I didn't promote our services.

If anything, I fell out of marketing.

Intuitive Marketer Principle 7: Know your niche and be consistent

- ☐ Be clear about the specific niche you are targeting
- ☐ Get inside the head of the typical representation of this niche
- ☐ Unpack the demographic of your niche, needs, wants
- ☐ Get emotional – what are the fears and aspirations of your niche market?
- ☐ Build trust through language, your story (how it relates to theirs) and empathy
- ☐ Maintain trust, build a brand your niche recognises
- ☐ Be consistent with the brand

We started off aiming for the wrong target market for our skills set. Once we were in alignment with the right target markets, our intuition served us well and we took educated risks to give them what they wanted. We built a brand.

It is just as important to build a brand today, especially in a busy marketplace. Create a brand that reaches out into the offline as well as online world. Align your brand to the motivations and values of your target market.

CHAPTER 4

THE CREATIVE BRAIN

"Entrepreneurship is first of all, the power to create"
– Michael E Gerber

Intuitive Marketer Principle 8: Be creative. Do something different. If it works, let it become your signature trademark.

Intuitive Marketer Principle 9: Be different, be visible, be unique - use your creative brain

It was the metrosexual nineties, yet to me, the staff development officer looked like he'd stepped out of the seventies. In my viewpoint he was radical. He challenged the status quo and his motto was "dare to be different". He is probably one of the greatest influences in my life alongside the fifty-something salesman who told my twenty-something self that I could achieve anything I set myself out to do. It was the dare to be different statement that gave me permission to revisit the freedom loving, adventurous teenager inside of me.

On reflection, it wasn't an accident that we were a market leader. We worked hard. Sifting through what seemed like reams of pink tissue paper, we would take it in turns to read Agence Europe, a daily French newsletter, reporting updates from the European Institutions. Between notices about foot and mouth disease, the Information Super Highway and high definition television, we kept up to date with European policy development. The interest was simple. Consultation led to green and white papers, which led to the Policy. Policy led to financial instruments, e.g. grants, leading to great opportunity to organise conferences and workshops. Also, policy interested us as subject matter for our conferences.

Even though we were bound by the rules and regulations of the university, we had some freedom not bound by academic rigour. We were considered maverick by some of our colleagues in the department to which we belonged. Our professional development programs didn't have to be approved by academic resource committees. Our programs were vocational, and we used practitioners to pass on their skills, knowledge, and wisdom.

Banishing Fear

We were ground breaking. We rose to new opportunities. We developed programs that people wanted. We also sought advice and approached the presenters and workshop leaders with credibility and experience. The European Briefing Officer, the Head of the Unit, was a non-conformist with an incredible history as a young European Liberal. She told us unofficial stories that I would be surprised if they were in the public domain today. She told us the private stories behind some of the major developments in the European Community. It was her connections that led to some of the most memorable events such as our role in the organisation of the Regional Summit of the Mayors of Europe in 1992, on the eve of the Single European Market and the fact-finding study visit to Bruges and Brussels by a group of Swedish MP's prior to Sweden deciding to apply to join the European Union.

The Regional Summit was probably a baptism of fire for our secretary. It was her second major event, but the first of this magnitude. Our participants, Mayors, were significantly powerful in local government in their municipalities across Europe. She was especially nervous the day we met up with our Scottish organising partners for the first time. We were waiting for a planning meeting in the foyer of the prestigious

Caledonian Hotel in Edinburgh where the conference would take place. It was being used for a convention of black-suited businessmen and the level of testosterone was high. I suggested she observe these men preening their hair as they talked. It was a sort of ritual. She began to relax and I saw a laughter, smile on her face when I added that she might imagine them with wives or girlfriends back home who would whip them back into shape. It's amazing how the imagination can still the fears of the brain. She was relaxed by the time our meeting started and went on to enjoy the jovial yet competitive camaraderie of the Edinburgh and Glasgow conference partners that persisted right through to the event itself. It would have been very embarrassing if somebody hadn't have noticed the event logo on the main screen was upside down the night before the conference. It would have shown the event in Glasgow not Edinburgh. The Glaswegian thought it was hilarious.

We could have been intimidated by the thought of people in positions of power who we worked with over the years. In reality, they are just human and respond well to a normal conversation. We found that even though the Mayors had high status in their municipalities, they were polite, ordinary people who welcomed our customer service, especially to overcome differences in language and culture.

Showcasing Innovation

"Innovation distinguishes between a leader and a follower" – Steve Jobs

When it came to being creative, we were as creative as British people could be. We weren't into the touchy-feely stuff, but we got quite creative in the design of workshops. We clearly applied the difference between a keynote presentation and workshop facilitation. Our workshops were designed to be interactive. We relished the idea of building projects or activities as we went along. We welcomed creative ideas and sometimes had to be creative in what we did.

What would be examples of the most creative episodes I could think of? There are two instances that stand out. One that delivered what we had promised and the second as an example of lateral thinking. Both are behind the scenes examples of the lengths we went to in order to deliver exceptional customer service.

What do you do when an important showcase keynote demonstrating new technology gets withdrawn two days before a conference? It was the early 1990s. This was an IT conference for education where we were going to demonstrate satellite technology. It should have been simple. We had a video conference room booked at the European Commission. We would be talking to the presenter via satellite from Brussels (Belgium) to our venue in Bradford (UK). What could go wrong?

Two days before the conference, we got a call from the European Commission telling us that as there were only two rooms with video conferencing equipment and one had been taken out of use for redecoration. The Agriculture Ministers had pulled rank and were taking our booked room. We were committed to delivering our audience what they were expecting but couldn't really argue with the Agriculture Minsters. These were the days when email was very new, satellite technology was still an innovation and the World Wide Web was in its early days. We had lost our star attraction.

I phoned every place I could think of that might have access to satellite technology, including a schools' education satellite project at the University of Plymouth. They could help but it was going to cost us a lot of money; money we did not have in the budget. We were running out of time. The day before the conference I received a phone call from somebody who was a regular attendee of our events. We had developed a small family of followers. Even in those days we had our version of raving fans. He heard a note of despondency in my voice and asked what was wrong. I told him. He asked me to give him a few minutes. True to his word he rang me back in what seemed like no time. He had secured the Plymouth people for free as his partner was on their team. I would never have guessed the link because he worked for a council in Wales and Plymouth is on the South Coast of England. The only catch was that we would need to move the angle of the satellite on the rooftop of the university. The satellite engineer was called in and I left work for the day to look after my children and prepare for the speakers' meal that night. I rang the secretary later in the afternoon and was told the European Briefing Officer was on the roof, helping the satellite engineer move the satellite, using safety equipment and all. How's that for dedication to duty?

In addition to moving the satellite dish, we had to improvise with the cables. Luckily the satellite receiving equipment was on our office floor level, but we had to hang cables from the satellite room, across a foyer area, out of the office of one of the professors down to the lecture theatre below. Today we would probably not be allowed to contravene safety guidelines, but our participants got their demonstration, although improvised, and they knew nothing of the mayhem going on in the background. Creative customer service at its best. At the time, we were showcasing innovation. Today we have the luxury of Wi-Fi, webinar software and mobile phone apps.

Simple but Effective

We were also creative in what we did. We invested in the latest upgrades of computers and software, applying what we learnt into our marketing processes. This allowed us to put our own creativity into action.

Intuitive Marketer Principle 8: Be creative. Do something different. If it works, let it become your signature trademark.

- ☐ If what you've done so far doesn't work, create your way out of a problem.
- ☐ Learn to think outside the box. Practice by taking one element from a process you are familiar with and seek to get around this omission.
- ☐ The best solution to competition is to create something new (e.g. product, innovation, process, promise)

Sometimes we needed to be creative from within. It was a couple of days before a conference. We still didn't have all the information from the presenters and I was getting frustrated that we couldn't finish off the participant packs as we liked to include background information about the sessions and the presenters. I decided to write a limerick. I took it to the fax machine and sent it to the presenters. Within an hour I had all the information I wanted and some jovial presenters and workshop leaders at the conference. It can take one simple but effective quirky action that will stand out in the perceptions of people who then gravitate toward your business.

The Creative Mind Set

The twenty-something me would describe creativity as eye-catching visuals on brochures, magazines, the Yellow Pages, and newspapers; something that would capture the eye of the reader. Specifically, she would be painfully aware of the power of the image and the written word and what it can evoke, but without the confidence or imagination to explore the potential. In my thirties, I would describe creativity as being entrepreneurial. I would look around for opportunity and act on it to propose new conference and workshop ideas. This version of me developed the ability to look beyond the norm and reach out to new possibilities for innovation, a skill I have honed and use with my clients today.

I currently work with clients who want to step up above and beyond what they are doing. They have a vision but are blocked by self-doubt and lack of support from others. I have a talent for knowing and applying my intuition to enhance my mentoring program. It's amazing what people can do with simple changes to the way they approach things; they even win awards. One mentee, a CEO of a small not-for-profit, had spent 10 years looking for additional space for her programs to no avail. Their facility was bursting at the seams. The local council was a barrier; they were not interested as there were other similar organisations in the area and she couldn't get anybody to take up her case. We worked on her own mind-set featuring entrepreneurial insights and habits of successful business people. She got creative. She watched how others worked and did the same. She was successful in applying for a few hundred thousand dollars for just one community project, not to forget the others she had in her arsenal. Today her organisation operates a community projects hub leased from the local council with access to an additional training room. It is right across the road from the main facility. When she got creative from the inside out, things started to happen in her favour.

The creative me of today still does not have any drawing skills, but is even more aware of the need for being creative and to stand out in a crowded marketplace. Is the marketplace really more crowded today than it was thirty years ago (remember when phone directories and the Yellow Pages were really useful chunky door stops when we weren't using them to source plumbers, marketers and just about anything under the sun)? Or are too many people promoting in one stagnant ocean of sameness?

How many business coaches are promoting their services just like their neighbour, using similar techniques on social media and email? How do you filter out which ones to follow when they are all selling you the same dream? I have an email address that I use only for signing up to webinars and downloads, which I know will be followed by a flood of emails for further promotions. I can then easily filter the ones I get fed up with, which then go straight to junk mail or get unsubscribed. However, I do tend to move mail back to my inbox if I've seen the author face-to-face and value their work. There's a lesson here for online marketers to value face-to-face interactions as a way to gain long term trust and engagement.

Why do we need to be creative and what do we need to do to be creative today?

There are some extremely successful people on social media and equally there are as many who have lost a lot of money trying to engage in a marketplace where there is already a plethora of market leaders. The market leaders create a strong brand, the rest must compete on price, quality, and point of difference. Sounds very much like Michael Porter's Generic Competitive Strategies in practice. If you can't compete on price, then take the eye of the customer away from the price.

When it comes to price, enter the sales funnel with gurus suggesting we introduce products and services from $7 incrementally to high end ticket offerings. It goes something like this.

- Option A - Start by offering something for free (e.g. Checklist, e-book guide) that leads to a webinar, a workshop, or a conversation with a marketing expert. Upsell to a $247-$497 or even $997 online program that leads to a $10,000+ service.
- Option B – Create a $7-$47 item or e-book that leads to a $27-$97 per month subscription that can be upgraded to gold and platinum options

These are examples of funnel marketing strategies that work because of the creation of trust and hopefully some face-to-face contact along the way. For quality, and to avoid competing on low prices, we are advised to add value by loading up the item for sale with additional free bonuses. Who can avoid a bargain?

But the point of difference is another thing. I once sat in a network meeting when the guest presenter went around the room asking people what their point of difference was. This would have been a good exercise had it not been that he got it wrong. He did a sixty second pitch about what he does and nothing about his point of difference. When we check the website content for clients, we note that not many show their point of difference to the visitor who lands on their site on a mission to find the supplier who stands out by reaching out to them with a point of difference from the crowd. Some websites don't even tell the visitor where they are or where they service.

How do you stand out in the sea of sameness? It's not too difficult if you get very clear on who would benefit from your product or service if you could make them feel good as a result? Start thinking. Who are they, where do they hang out, not just on the internet and find a way to get their attention. What language do they use? This is where creativity separates the movers and shakers from the pack. I realised after three years that if I carried on listening to the same things, I would be in danger of settling in as a member of the pack. The entrepreneurial, younger me, would be horrified. She was creative and would find opportunity by looking outside the box and daring to be different. I have a point of difference for each of my services. For my grant writing services, I have worked on both sides of the funding fence on TWO continents. For my partnership services, I have developed a UNIQUE package based on 20 years working with partnership ventures both in the private and community sectors. For my marketing services, I have wisdom based on my epic journey which has also embraced the evolution of technology alongside decades of practical offline marketing strategies. This wisdom enables me to explain the value of adopting today's marketing tools as part of an underlying strategy.

Intuitive Marketer Principle 9: Be different, be visible, be unique - use your creative brain
- ☐ Find out about your competitors – their characteristics and strengths
- ☐ Find and exploit the gap in their product, service, or delivery
- ☐ Identify unique opportunities to promote your message
- ☐ What other ways can you stand out from your competition?

The ones who stand out from the crowd are the ones who exercise their creative mind. They overcome fear of the unknown, make things happen and engage with their target market. Creative thinking for success is not a new concept. The book "The Science of Getting Rich" by Wallace D. Wattles focuses on creativity over competition as a determinant of financial success. If you're not convinced, read it.

CHAPTER 5

CRUISING THE INFORMATION SUPER HIGHWAY

"High-capacity fibre optic networks will be the information superhighway of tomorrow"

– Al Gore

Intuitive Marketer Principle 10: Changes in technology move fast. Harness technology as an innovator and keep an eye out for new developments.

Intuitive Marketer Principle 11: Harness the power of technology to stay ahead of the competition

Today it's almost impossible to avoid the internet. Facebook is currently the most sophisticated marketing engine in the world. Social media and the dotcom revolution have made billionaires out of ordinary people. People research on the internet before they make buying decisions. We carry the internet in our pockets. It's so easy to be carried away on this giant wave, but it wasn't always like this.

My journey into the digital age started with the teenage me. I decided to study for a Computer Studies 'O' Level qualification as an extracurricular course in my final year at school in England. As Computer Studies was an innovation, I travelled across town, as did students from the other schools in the district, to after-school lessons. My sister was a student of that school and studied this course at the same time as part of her normal studies. The course was based around binary coding and we wrote and sent home-made programs to one of only two organisations in town (the tax office and an insurance company) that housed rooms full of computers. We had to wait two weeks to find out if we'd made a mistake in our simple programming. I got it. I passed easily and therein started a lifetime of being stalked by technology. It was also at this time that I became familiar with the phrase "necessity is the mother of invention", a term used to qualify the stories behind the introduction of the first computers and which could justify the rise of the technological age. I'm not sure where that statement sits today as we sit on the verge of AI and robots redefining the workplace.

Looking back, my life from analogue to digital started when I decided to take a secretarial course in the sixth form at school as the rebel in me was not interested in going to university at that time. So, I spent two years learning shorthand and touch typing on manual typewriters. My second job introduced me to electronic typewriters, telex machines – both manual and tape machines - and the advent of visual display units (VDU's) linked to a central mainframe computer. Marketing materials were still printed professionally because photocopying machines were not the sophisticated multi-function machines of today. One day I found a relatively unused machine gathering dust in a storage room. It intrigued me. When I asked what it was, nobody could tell me until the sales manager told me that it was a machine that would copy the content of A4 sheets that could be transmitted to a similar machine at other sites, including our Grimsby raw material supply site. It was sitting there because nobody knew how to use it. It had been bought to make our ordering process simpler. Instead, I had been using a telex machine for two years without knowing the existence of this 'fax' machine. I wasn't frightened of this technology and I quickly got the hang of it. It saved me 50 minutes every Friday afternoon.

Only three years ago I was working on an IT project with an aged care service provider. They had had a bank of six iPads stashed away in a cupboard for two years because people were afraid to use them. We have clients that are reluctant to use the full features of Facebook for marketing, and others that are reluctant to send out e-newsletters because of the threat of being accused of spamming. The biggest barrier to using new technology be it equipment or software, is fear.

The advent of the 1980s gave rise to VDUs (visual display units) which were screens attached to a mainframe computer system elsewhere, not the stand-alone PC we are familiar with today. The twenty-something me was a young mum employed by a temporary employment agency. I had made the conscious decision to work part-time on contracts whilst my children were young because I realised even then that technology was beginning to move fast and I needed to stay in the game. I was introduced to a wide diversity of programs, accessible through VDU's. No two programs were the same. There was a gap in the market for a one size fits all model that Microsoft went on to fill.

In my early twenties, I was introduced to the database side of marketing. It started with working on contracts to input the electoral roll of the whole of the UK into the computer system of a prominent catalogue company. This was building a database from scratch big time. The more details we input (accurately), the more we earned. I learnt to type very fast. Another contract at the same place saw me inputting the details of people who had subscribed to a miracle diet pill via newspaper advertisements. There was plenty of work if we wanted it, which fitted well around my evenings and weekends.

This analogue to digital system was innovative in its day. The catalogue company was a marketing harvesting machine of its day in that it used its giant computer system to collect people's information for marketing purposes. Not surprisingly, people wanting weight loss was then, is now, and will continue to be, a lucrative market.

In quick time, smaller businesses also began to use computer technology to collect their own customer data on electronic databases. I was in demand and kept busy with a variety of data input assignments. The mid 80's was the turning point for converting customer records to online databases. In one assignment, I was inputting data for a car sales company that recorded the exchange of chickens as one thousand-pound deposits towards the purchase of a car. Don't ask.

Surprisingly, why do so many businesses today not have a customer database, and if they do, why are they not using it? We work with training organisations that collect student data for government reporting, but have never thought to use data to engage further with these customers. Not too long ago, a business client gave us his database to survey customers. He gave us written diaries going back six years. We did contact these customers and found that there had been opportunities to refer to friends or sell more products, but the contact details of the supplier had been lost and there had been no contact from him in the meantime.

It's so much easier today to collect and use customer data. There is no excuse for not knowing what the customer wants and responding accordingly.

A Historic Milestone

It was only after the birth of my fourth child that I took 15 enjoyable months out of the workplace. Although money was tight, it wasn't a major issue and we even managed to have a family holiday. When we got back, I started to question whether I should go back to work. I decided to leave it to chance. I applied for two positions and got two interviews before I broke my ankle. When I rang to cancel, the second organisation said they'd come to me. This was the university and the door opened to an amazing job which allowed me to travel as well as witness historic. This period in my life started with the 'fall of the wall' in November 1989, signalling the start of German Reunification. This was very week I started my role in the European Briefing Unit.

1989 was also the year of the invention of the World Wide Web and the beginning of the next stage of my technology journey. It would take a few years before the influence of the World Wide Web would reach the university, so let's get first things first. Starting at the university, I was introduced to the stand-alone PC. Word and Word

Perfect were in competition with each other and Courier was the only font available until Times New Roman provided a welcome relief. We used 80286 machines with Microsoft Word and 5.25-inch floppy disks, progressing to 3.5-inch disks in time. Despite using discs on multiple machines, we didn't really suffer from virus attacks. I became familiar with the DOS computer operating language and still refer to it even today for basic troubleshooting.

I was working in a university that already had access to the internet via the Joint Academic Network (JANET). We had email using Pine and online access to European Commission databases. Although we were limited in who we could send emails to, we were able to keep up to date with European developments through the ECHO and Eurobases databases. These were useful sources for us to gather information that we could use to keep our participants informed of new opportunities. We were accessing information by online text gateways. Online graphic user interface information databases were still being developed for the commercial market, spearheaded by news and financial services companies.

1993 changed my world. On the European stage, President of the European Community, Jacques Delors, presented the ground breaking white paper "Growth, Competitiveness, Employment: The Challenges and Ways Forward into the 21st Century" which included a large section on the development of a Community-wide common information area and led to a strategy for developing an information society. This was visionary and an amazingly accurate prediction.

In those days, most of what we take for granted today was just a vision. In the Information Society, there would be more jobs and new jobs for working from home. Distance learning online would enhance lifelong learning in a changing society and city information highways would bring the Information Society into the home. Our ability to work from home, keep updating our skills and knowledge through webinars and information downloads and the fact that we can access the extensive internet from our homes was a vision is a fantastic outcome of the leading fathers, not forgetting Al Gore, who first used the term "Information Super Highway" connecting the world's computer networks to create the infrastructure for global growth.

In December 1993, a colleague and I went into one of the student computer labs and had our first encounter with the World Wide Web. We accessed a South Pole expedition Christmas message using an innovative graphical interface search engine called Mosaic. Instead of lines of green or orange text, we were looking at a colourful image. In the New Year, our PCs were quickly updated to include this new technology and before long I was learning HTML to put together a webpage for our unit. At the same time Microsoft was making big leaps with its operating systems and we were introduced to the Office suite. We had long since moved from Pine to an email client called Simeon. Now we were able to use Outlook and Outlook Express. PowerPoint has replaced transparent slides that were either copied from documents via a photocopier or drawn upon in situ. Today's presentations are far more sophisticated and extend to video, something unimaginable in those days.

Today we take program families such as Microsoft Office for granted with little awareness of how integrated software packages opened up the marketing world at a simple and cost-effective level. Without them, we wouldn't be talking about email marketing, making powerful presentations, and using webinars and videos, creating and using databases and generating creative advertising copy. Microsoft and other software giants were allowing us to keep more control of our marketing operations and lower costs by keeping them in-house.

Pioneering Technology

It was also about this time when I got into attending the annual Online Exhibition at Olympia in London. Held in December each year, it ran at the same time as the London Office of the European Commission's annual presentation to invited stakeholders; a perfect opportunity to keep up to date with the latest trends on the European scene at the same time as the latest updates on information technology. This was one day of the year I always looked forward to.

When I first attended the Online Exhibition, it was dominated by well-known news agencies selling online access to news or information databases. CD Rom drives were becoming features of new generation PCs, starting with information access only and then the development of the CDi which opened up interactive engagement. At the time, the DVD was still a couple of years away from success. It was interesting to talk to stall holders who would talk about the progress they were making, but that they could only record minutes of film onto video and had not yet got the capability of recording full feature films. Today we use cloud technology. We live stream TV and video. Information is available any time we choose. Opportunities for online and digital marketing have come a long way since the 1990s.

All of this exposure to the roll out of information technology advancements was bound to lead to opportunities for conferences. So, we obliged. We started with IT conferences for teachers. One comment I remember at the plenary of the conference with the satellite demonstration mentioned earlier, was from a teacher who commented that email was a good idea but how could education adopt new technology with yesterday's budgets? Today, education is at the forefront of investment in technology. The forty-something me was also an expert in facilitating educational webinars and online classrooms. I worked in a regional office for adult community education. We had a Moodle e-learning platform as far back as 2004, which came in very useful during the 2006/7 bushfires in North East Victoria. We had a community forum space on the platform that was being used by subscribers caught in the fires as a way to keep in contact with their 'community' colleagues. Today there are a plethora of community forums within Facebook itself. Only a dozen years ago, community forums were not as commonly accessible.

Today, there appear to only be a handful of commercially available webinar platforms that people widely use. Even though webinars are supposed to convert at 10%, much higher than any other conversion method, the software available to business is basic compared to the webinar platforms used in education. Commercial webinars allow for replays through additional software add on apps. They allow presenters to show slides and can respond to questions. There is a large focus on the marketing end of the webinar software, to promote and get people to the webinar. Webinar platforms designed for education are far more advanced in available features. They allow presenters to set up individual sessions or whole courses. These courses can also be sold online. Webinar presenters can flick between presentation slides, documents, websites and just about anything. They are not confined to presentation slides. Education-based webinar platforms also include breakout rooms. The ideal webinar software client should be somewhere between the marketing and education driven platforms, but simple enough to overcome the fear factor experienced by technophobes.

Another concept of the 1990s was "cyberspace". In 1996, we organised a two-day conference in Manchester, England, simply called "Learning in Cyberspace". It attracted participants from thirteen countries. With topics such as telematics for education and training, superhighways for education, educational software and multimedia, technology in the classroom and new vision of lifelong learning, people were hungry for the promise that information technology could deliver. We had found the hungry crowd and through our networks and marketing channels, we were the focal point to quench that hunger.

The entrepreneurial, working mum, had harnessed a good marketing strategy through the development of the very premise, which successful marketers of today rely on. I had monitored the development of the internet and information technology by attending networking meetings and ground-breaking expo's. We had translated this knowledge into opportunities and benefits for education. We worked with (joint venture) partners with networks across Europe and attracted around 200 participants from thirteen countries. What we didn't do was follow-up afterwards. Today, I would see that as a basic missed opportunity.

> **Intuitive Marketer Principle 10: Changes in technology move fast. Harness technology as an innovator and keep an eye out for new developments.**
> - How can you use technology in your business?
> - What difference will technology make to your productivity and/profit generation activities
> - What skills do you need to understand and/or use technology?
> - What technology processes do you need to outsource (internally or externally)?
> - What new technology is coming that you should investigate to assist with your business activities?

A New Beginning

I thought I had escaped from technology when I emigrated to Australia, but I was wrong. I landed in a job that found me in the e-learning space. I was leading projects on using technology to assist with learning in adult education. We had a Moodle e-learning platform as far back as 2004, and worked on government funded pilot projects using GPS, digital storytelling, and podcasting. I was facilitating webinars in the education space before they became popular in the business space. Move over iTunes. Our projects were at the cutting edge of podcasting.

So, with all that experience behind me, why did I find myself peddling fast to catch up over the last few years. How did I take my eye off the ball?

On hindsight, I wasn't peddling to catch up. I was adapting my mind set. I was being taught a new lesson. For years, educational institutions grappled with the opportunities of e-learning. It was difficult to persuade teachers to adopt technology skills sets. E-Learning was not an imperative and I felt frustrated about the level of general resistance. Money was being invested in an education sector that wasn't ready for change. Sadly, for some, this is still the case today.

Conversely, the introduction of webinar technology, iTunes, YouTube, and learning engagement tools was met by entrepreneurial innovators and a hungry crowd in the business sector. Webinars are now being delivered with education content with opportunities to follow through to the next level. Businesses are now sharing with other businesses the skills they need to grow. Recordings of online and face-to-face training are kept on YouTube and other video storage platforms. I honestly think a new education revolution is coming; one led by business and entrepreneurs who are turning learning upside down through video, webinars, and online communities.

Education is struggling to catch up and somewhere along the way, businesses are likely to take over the role of education from institutions that are wrapped up in the red tape of quality standards for education and training. What's the point of a heavily structured and monitored training program for a qualification when businesses can access information, skills and training from each other on demand? The Internet of Things, the next generation of technology, could take this even further by analysing people's skills through usage of digital equipment, and designing custom made training.

Businesses are now offering online education from skills and experience, not academic premise. Is it any wonder universities are now offering courses online for free?

Intuitive Marketer Principle 11: Harness the power of technology to stay ahead of the competition
- ☐ What technology is your competition using to generate business and deliver products and services to the customer?
- ☐ Where are the technology gaps?
- ☐ What would it take to incorporate the technology that the competition is not yet using, into your own business (include cost benefits)?
- ☐ What new technology innovations can you incorporate in your business model?

THE INTUITIVE MARKETER

Technology is now moving at such a fast pace, that anybody who doesn't keep up will be left behind. The visionaries of a generation ago could not have predicted how the Information Age has moved as quickly as it has to surpass even their wildest dreams. We have come a long way from using computers to record and sell information, to using tablets, PCs, and mobile devices to access social media and websites for marketing and delivery of products and services.

Recently, a client commented that he was pleased that I run with the pack when it comes to new technological innovations, rather than being in the group behind. He meant well. I prefer to herd the hunting pack, pointing them in the right direction.

When it comes to technology, it would be foolish not to stay hungry.

CHAPTER 6

BUILDING A COMMUNITY

"Permission marketing is marketing without interruptions"
- Seth Godin

Intuitive Marketer Principle 12: Keep your focus on the problem you are solving for the client in front of you, right up to the point of delivery

Intuitive Marketer Principle 13: In the digital age, the currency of genuine trust should incorporate old world offline strategies

A successful business is one that builds a community of customers that will be loyal, will stay with the business in hard times and will become its ambassadors. When I started my business I only had a small number of clients, so I didn't think I even needed to focus on building a list of customers who would become my community. As I changed my business model, it became clear that I would need to build communities of people interested in our services. Good idea, but how do we achieve this level of success? I turned to my own experience to help me through the minefield of available advice that goes from how to build organic lists to sharing or buying other people's lists.

Visibility

The last thing a business wants is to be given a reputation as a spammer and have its online mailing and newsletter accounts closed down. For this reason, buying ready-made mailing lists doesn't work in the same way that building a list of people who have had some connection with the business does. It is vital to acquire and build a customer database organically based on permission.

In order to start a community, it's important to niche and target the people and businesses who will benefit from your products or services. Once the niche has been identified, the challenge is to communicate your value proposition and to nurture their interest by keeping them engaged. It is about being visible to prospects at the point of need and to get them to buy your products and services when they are ready. For this, you will need a database.

There are a plethora of online tools and strategies to get people to declare their interest (such as contact forms, download buttons, and calendar appointments), but these can't happen unless the prospective buyer is attracted to your proposition. This is the bigger challenge; not the online tools. The community that my thirty-something served was built on face-to-face contact. People knew us. We had credibility. We were visible. Today I find myself on a growing number of database mailing lists. I filter those I am interested in, preferring those people I have seen in live action, then those who I have seen presenting via video or webinar. If I don't like the webinar, follow-up emails go to junk. I have been sub-consciously selecting the emails I want to read via this process.

Do you get emails while you're asleep? Do you find that most of them are sales promotion related? Do you get the seven-a.m. flurry of emails into your inbox? These are examples of businesses timing their emails to be most visible such as when people wake up and check their mobile phones. I now relegate most of these to my junk mail box because there are simply too many to read. They are no longer as visible as they used to be and my interest in being part of their community has waned. Unfortunately, I am now receiving SMS texts. If only there was a SMS junk filter.

What other ways are there to be visible at the point of need for your community? One way would be to host impromptu webinars, Facebook, or YouTube Live events on a hot topic as it occurs. Or to reward loyalty with incentives so that you are top of mind when they make purchasing decisions. We occasionally send out coffee or tea bags as part of our "have one on us" campaign to selected clients. They love it. When was the last time you received something in the mail that wasn't a bill or something you purchased yourself?

Trust

Underpinning any community of loyal customers is trust. Trust is based on confidence that the seller is genuinely interested in helping the customer; that they understand the customer and help them with the results they are looking for. Once established, customers will support the business until the trust is broken. Even through difficult times, customers will not move away and will defend the business. Car manufacturers attract buyers who stay with the brand even if it is a point of ridicule. I know, because, whilst studying for my Education Marketing Diploma, on the advice of the lecturer I submitted two marketing campaign ideas to a car company. One idea was based on the car company's poor image, yet loyal fan base.

The first campaign idea was based on the Bohemian history of the car and re-emerging Eastern European economies, and the second focused on the loyal customer base who had put up with jokes about the quality of the car even though it had dramatically improved in recent times.

I got the standard "we have our marketing team who know what they're doing" response. Two years later a familiar campaign appeared on television. I wrote and queried the origin and was told that the marketing team members had changed since my submission and to send copies of the original correspondence. At the time, we were packing to emigrate and I did not have access to the documents.

Over dinner one evening we told the story to friends and said if the second campaign rolls out, it would be too much of a co-incidence. Just before we left the UK… guess what? A second coincidence.

The second campaign was responsible for relaunching the brand and turning the brand image around in the perception of the public. It was built on a loyal customer base. I did not find the documents until a couple of years later. I still have them, but did not follow up at the time; a long-term regret.

Fortunately for the European Briefing Unit, trust was in high supply. It was based on our consistent approach, values, and brand. Anybody who came to any of our workshops would be guaranteed of our style of delivery. We would engage practitioners, including ourselves where we had the expertise. My role in delivery moved from organisation to also facilitation in my later days of working in the Unit. When somebody first told me, I would be out there presenting I replied categorically not. I was horrified. I had no interest in presenting in public. The me of today, just loves to be in front of the crowd, getting people talking and waiting for the ah ha expressions that invariably light up faces.

Likewise, our conferences would include a mix of policy and practice. We consistently got participation from the European Institutions, which leveraged our engagement of other policy makers. We were also consistently successful in getting our events promoted in the European Commission UK newsletter. Already alluded to, we put a high value on social engagement, which included paying for speakers' accommodation and a pre-event dinner. We paid a lot of attention to the quality of food, not just speakers' meals, but workshop and conference meals as well.

We incorporated evening dinners into events of two-days or more. Watching people change with the assistance of food is a social phenomenon to witness. We would observe people turn up for two-day plus events not knowing anybody or just one person at the most. For the first day, people would gravitate to their sole colleagues or people they had met at the table or a breakout session. The evening meal would shake up these limited alliances with the help of an alcoholic beverage or three. By the next day, the atmosphere was very much a "friends with all" feeling. By the time they departed, many people had grown their networks considerably. Translate this practice to our organised study visits to Brussels, with its quality fine dining and respect for wines that match the many courses, and our participants went home with happy memories, not just about the content and learnings of the visit, but also the social camaraderie. Throughout all these experiences, the staff went by the adage "family eat last". We made sure there was enough food for all; otherwise we would have to do without. Food was a cornerstone of our success in gaining trust.

The one time 'trust' had a negative impact on us was not directly our fault. On this occasion, we organised a study visit to Brussels for a group of teachers from Bedfordshire. Unfortunately, the first day of the visit coincided with the very day the mad cow disease crisis hit the headlines. The hotel we were staying in obviously didn't trust the source of its meat. For our evening meal on the first night, instead of lamb, we were fed beef. If there was going to be a problem with the beef, then we were fair game.

Quality and Expectations

With favourable food experiences, the overall feedback on our event evaluation forms was positive. Yes, we did get some bad reviews (you can't please everybody all the time), but we did follow up on the trends. Our evaluation forms covered presentation, content, and operations. We strove to keep improving. I sometimes wonder about the current trend to rate venues, accommodation, and experiences online. Getting negative feedback can be soul destroying and once out there for the world to see, it must be more difficult to get back credibility. Badly timed poor ratings can destroy a business without giving it the opportunity to resolve systemic issues.

I don't believe it is ultimately productive to use ratings apps as widely as they are being used online today. Firstly, they are subjective and secondly, if somebody does have a poor experience, normal conditions of continuous improvement apply feedback to assist with improving the service provided. One piece of negative feedback amplifies ten times greater than one piece of positive feedback. Thanks to internet trolls, one negative review can greatly damage a business far more than one positive review can boost its reputation. At least we had the chance to rectify issues, whilst maintaining and building trust, without looking over our shoulders.

In this digital age, in addition to food, we also tend to forget another basic principle of what makes a quality customer experience. Some business and marketing experts who deliver face-to-face workshops operate on the principle of people attending because they are attracted to the benefits and results. There is no additional step between payment and delivery of the presentation. Many don't even think to ask the attendees what they specifically want from the event.

Each group has a different focus depending on the mix of existing skills and needs. Those who sell well from the stage, scoop the low hanging fruit, and then follow the rest up with a phone call. Would their success-rate improve even further if they included the feedback from a pre-event survey into the delivery of the presentation? For us, the pre-course questionnaire helped us focus our presentation and message, improving the experience and satisfaction of the attendees. Our presenters were prepared and focused. People thought they were talking directly to them.

As technology is evolving, the opportunity to survey prospects is becoming easier. Autoresponder software allows for questionnaires. Google has a free 'Forms' function for online surveys. Webinar presenters can now carry out polls. There is no excuse for not delivering a quality experience based on the needs and wants of the people in the group.

Intuitive Marketer Principle 12: Keep your focus on the problem you are solving for the client in front of you, right up to the point of delivery

☐ What is the client's problem that you are solving?

☐ What are you offering to solve this problem (value proposition)?

☐ How well are you communicating this solution: to the customer, staff and delivery partners?

☐ Is the value proposition at the forefront of product or service design?

☐ Is the value proposition consistently a part of the delivery of the product or service?

The Power is in the List

How many times have we heard the phrase *"the money is in the list"*? We are constantly being bombarded with advice that we should build our databases to increase our chances of sales.

Talk to any internet marketing guru and they'll tell you the key to securing clients is to nurture trust with the aim of getting people voluntarily onto your mailing list. It can be a convoluted process and involves autoresponder software and a marketing funnel. It depends on the business owner becoming a master of, or engaging an expert in, using autoresponders, a customer relationship management system (CRM) and marketing funnels.

Our customers were satisfied. We knew that because we held a unique position of credibility with our participants. We had the database to beat all databases (well, that's my personal opinion). This is how it worked at the time before autoresponders and CRMs. Trained in DOS we typed up mailing lists for local government, quangos, education, voluntary sector, and community development organisations. We were able to interchange job positions. We targeted the appropriate job roles for our events. We printed out letters through mail merge and labels for envelopes. There was nothing out of the ordinary with this simple process. It would be slightly more complicated in today's online world.

The difference came with our Master List. In addition to the pre-course questionnaire and evaluation form, we handed out to our participants forms for people to subscribe to future events. We had opt-in even then. We even went as far as tick boxes for specific areas of general interest. Responses were added to our Master List database using Microsoft Access. Every January we would ask people on the list if they wished to remain or be removed. Here's the kicker.

Instead of removing people, our database grew. Very few wanted to be taken off the list. Not only did it grow, but we noticed that the people who were added to the list in the early days became senior managers and strategic influencers that we could use as expert practitioner facilitators for our workshops. They developed professional relationships with each other and created networks. We were able to tap into those networks at will. As they became managers, they would send their staff to our events and they in turn enrolled onto our Master List. Thus, started a second generation of networks that we were able to tap into. Our Master List was not excessively large, yet was big enough to generate significant repeat business and create networks within our network. They say the money is in the list, but we also had something more valuable than money. This was trust on steroids.

In a digital economy, we're taught to promote trust through nurturing into a sales funnel. Add social proof via testimonials. We had social proof in spades. It was already in our list and it was multi-dimensional. We had access to individual success, acquired expertise and networks, and it was unique in that it was home to an inter-generational mailing list. There was power in our list.

This was achieved in an analogue economy. I knew the power of trust borne through the wider customer experience. I also knew the power of mailing lists. What lessons can the present me learn against the digital backdrop?

THE LIFEBLOOD OF SUCCESS

Today, in my hunger for knowledge, I exchange my details for access to free reports. I go onto somebody's database expecting to be inundated with email messages trying to sell me the next offer. Rather than blocking my emails, I use one email address for this purpose. It is then easy for me to mark all emails in the mailbox as read or delete. Before I do, I scan down to see if there's an email of interest. My eyes are first drawn to those whom I have seen in person and whose presentations I enjoyed. If they are in the junk email I will move them over to my inbox and read them before deleting the rest. Why do I do this? It's because most of the one's I've visited have got my trust. The ones I've seen and don't get my trust are those who follow up with the hard sell and retreat when they realise that I don't have the thousands of dollars available to take up their life changing millionaire offer. The team that reaches out because they believe in what I'm doing and offers me an irresistible offer, will get my undying trust. I'm still waiting.

When it comes to online marketing, we are reaching saturation point. Instead of focusing on building mailing lists as profit generators, marketers could get to know who the people are on the list. There may be some powerful allies or somebody with something of value hiding in the list. We experienced a real-life version of this scenario, when we discovered that sitting in the audience of our environmental conference, was the one person with responsibility for millions of pounds (equivalent) for a European environmental fund. He was sitting incognito, gathering intelligence, listening to what people were saying. He introduced himself to us at the end of the event. Imagine contacts like him hiding in your mailing list.

Intuitive Marketer Principle 13: In the digital age, the currency of genuine trust should incorporate old world offline strategies

☐ What nurturing strategies are you using to generate trust online?
- o Newsletters
- o Education
- o Offers
- o Webinars
- o Social media groups
- o Other

☐ What nurturing strategies are you using to generate trust offline?
- o Face-to-face workshops
- o Referrals
- o Network meetings
- o Visits
- o Exhibitions/expo's – anywhere the prospect can meet you/your staff
- o Other

Today there is a large focus on developing trust in the online world, particularly in relation to nurturing prospects into becoming clients. Such is the focus, that it is easy to forget other, just as, if not more than, successful ways to build trust. Whilst it is tempting to sit behind a computer and build trust online – for some people this is preferable to feeling like wallflowers at network meetings, face-to-face contact unlocks long term trust in a way that online can't. Every business owner should belong to at least one face-to-face network; preferably one where potential customers hang out or where you can meet potential referral partners.

The winners of the future will be those who can wisely include analogue marketing such as networking, face-to-face activities and delivering an excellent customer experience, as well as build networks and trust online.

CHAPTER 7

BURN OUT

"Passion is energy. Feel the power that comes from focusing on what excites you" - *Oprah Winfrey*

Intuitive Marketer Principle 14: Build in time out - it doesn't have a negative impact on your productivity

In my networks, I come across thirty or forty-something women who are juggling it all; marriage, children, business, family, and social life. Some are trying to juggle it all and find themselves paying for time management counselling. It's like an infection. If we're not careful we succumb. It's not a modern-day disease. My own mother and grandmothers worked whilst managing their family lives. They worked in textile mills and auto part warehouses for ten-hour days. Their work was generally more physical. A lot of the conditions of work today incorporate computer and internet software into business strategy. We tend to be more cerebral, in constant battle with our feminine emotions.

As I observe my younger business acquaintances, I look back to me in my thirties and identify with the superwoman in each of them. I've been there and done that. Along the way I suffered from burn out. What I learnt was that when you don't enjoy what you're doing, either correct the cause or move on. It happened to me twice. I should have corrected the cause the first time it happened and I left my job the second time. I left a well-paid job and went into business and started a journey that could have led to information burn out, but for my previous experiences and the decision to write this book. I am now following my passion.

Superwoman

If you're a woman, you might relate to my story.

Instead of the expected transition to university, preferably Oxford or Cambridge (fortunately I can't carry the mantra of having had a tragic childhood, except to say I was a working-class scholar in a private grammar school with all that entails). I left school two weeks before the official end of the school year to start in full-time employment. I had no intention of going to university and stood by that decision until after my third daughter was born. I worked full time until I had my first child and in between the remaining four I worked part time. My husband wasn't well paid, so as a young mum I put a lot of pressure on myself to contribute to making ends meet. I worked flexibly, mornings or evenings with the wonderful support of family, especially my husband's grandparents. When I started working in the European Briefing Unit I had no idea of the journey I was embarking on. Twenty hours a week evolved to also include occasional weekends when we held weekend conferences in the early days. Before I knew it, I was travelling with overnight stays all over the UK, as well as to Brussels at least once or anything up to three times a year. Eventually I was working full time, but not until my youngest child was of school age.

After one trip away, I was asked by my mother, who had helped look after the children in my absence, exactly where I'd been. She wanted to know because my daughter's teacher had asked. My daughter had said somewhere beginning with B and that had started some guess work at school. Was it Birmingham? Or Bristol? Or Belfast? My daughter was correct. On that occasion, I had been to Brussels. It could have been any one of them.

Being involved in a successful growing venture was possible because of my extended family. However, it did overlap with my family life. I have a memory of getting back from the Lake District just in time for my daughter's birthday party and another one of flying to Brussels on the birthday of two of my other children. Over time these conflicts caught up with me.

After my youngest child was born, I had a strong desire to learn something new. I contacted the university's personnel department and was given the opportunity to study for an honours degree as a part time student, paid for by the university. I was ready to study, so of course I had to take it up, juggling my young family, growing responsibilities within the Unit and now studying for a degree. Superwoman or what?

Three years later our workshops and conferences were more prolific. I was working more hours, though not yet full time and I also graduated with my degree. I then decided to study for an education marketing diploma. It took me a bit longer than I anticipated to complete this one as I was over study by that point. This diploma didn't really teach me anything that I hadn't already learnt in my everyday job. For me the direction for my future learning was being set. From this point forward, my learning has been just in time and relevant to my needs. A new pattern was set for my marketing skills Renaissance.

Expanding Roles

As the success of the European Briefing Unit grew, roles and responsibilities became more complex. When I started, I was the part time secretary to the European Briefing Officer. Within two years I was organising events and setting up programs with a secretary; a good one at that. Two years later and we were assisted by a progression of work experience personnel ranging from three months to a year and including women returning to work, foreign exchange students and second chance college students. I had a special ability of being able to identify talents within 24 hours and thus setting up roles and responsibilities for these people to positively contribute to the

Unit's operations. One young man discovered he had a talent for numbers (co-incidentally, his dad was an accountant). Another used his new skills with PowerPoint presentations to present himself into a dream job. Carlos, a pony-tail wearing Spaniard who couldn't speak English without the aid of a dictionary when we first met, became fluent in English, and attracted a healthy female fan club. The students with strong research skills gravitated towards the European Briefing Officer who got them into researching policy and educational content. There was something for everybody.

Most, if not all, played a part in marketing and customer service (some even got to visit Brussels). We made sure that all were part of the on-the-day events team (the crew). Only once did we have a major issue. That was the occasion when a student on placement from the local college refused to assist the European Briefing Officer with hosting a dinner. It was only for one evening. We had a couple of back to back courses happening in London. I couldn't attend the first one, but would be available for the second. His religious beliefs prevented him from taking part in any meal where alcohol was served. Our dinners involved wine. Nobody was aware of this until it happened. Normally, we would have been able to work around it. It later transpired that he also had difficulties in taking orders from the other female staff. He had tolerated and respected me because he had been referred to me via a mutual male friend. Thankfully, he was the exception.

We were delivering 81 training days a year. That would be equivalent to just over two days a week direct contact as there was little training activity during school holidays. It wasn't as though we set up a full year program in advance. Our program was set up quarterly, except for the conferences which needed anything up to 18 months to organise. It was relentless.

At some point my ideal job became a burden. On hindsight, trying to do as much as we did, with me being the organising contact, was always going to lead to burn out. I am amazed it took as long as it did. I tried to get out a few times, but always missed out on the jobs I applied for. To be honest, I would have been thoroughly bored in those jobs, but didn't see that at the time. The day it really hit home that I had had enough was the day the Head of the Unit brought in a carrier bag full of receipts for expenses going back to the previous tax year and put it on my desk. As the organiser, my responsibility not only covered marketing, it also covered budgets and expenditure. I had my finger on the pulse of all profit and loss data for every event, within reason. I took two weeks' stress leave.

Time Management

The job was perfect. I was given enough responsibility, but I became toxic. Everything was a struggle whilst putting on a smiley face. I even had underlying post-natal depression that I did not address until my youngest daughter was thirteen. I had returned to work from maternity leave too soon and I had subsequently not taken enough time out for my own sanity. Even today, I am guilty of doing just the same, even though I know that there is a great deal of benefit from resting.

Ten years previously, as a busy young mum, I learnt the benefit of taking time out. Working in data input, I got paid on key depressions. Working evenings, I was able to supplement our family income by becoming a proficient typist. Fridays were quiet and instead of taking a 15-minute break, we were known to take up to 30 minutes. Incredibly, we did not lose key depressions and sometimes keyed more. Thus, proving that taking breaks boosts, not decreases, overall productivity.

Today, the gurus stress the importance of prioritising time out and holiday breaks. Guess what? They are right. If I had listened to the younger me, I would probably have enjoyed the role in the European Briefing Unit far longer than I did. I should not have taken work home with me. I should have taken time off in lieu of the additional hours worked. Easier said than done. Balance is the key.

My advice to anybody is to build time out into your calendar and use it. As a small business, it is so easy to work every spare hour you get, especially when you are working to deadlines. Try to avoid this practice. Stressed and burnt out does not make for the creative mind or good marketing decisions.

> **Intuitive Marketer Principle 14: Build in time out - it doesn't have a negative impact on your productivity**
> ☐ Set boundaries around your time – daily, weekly and monthly
> ☐ Take time out during the day for lunch and refreshment breaks (as you would in a job)
> ☐ Plan at least one week's vacation every three months – block out the dates as the first priority of your 90-day plan

I didn't listen to myself and nearly repeated the same pattern again in recent times.

As a business owner, it is not easy to switch off. I worked twenty-four seven in the early years. It is only now that I don't work weekends. I achieved this by weaning myself off working Saturdays first and then Sundays. I also learned how to close the office door and leave it closed.

Information Overload

At first, I attracted project work from people who knew me in my last job. This sustained me for the first couple of years and I didn't think to do any serious marketing. Work seemed to flow in easily. Not building marketing into the business from the beginning was a major mistake. By the time I realised this, work was beginning to dry up. My clients relied on grant funding to engage our services. Changes in state and federal governments led to a decline in the availability of funding and I realised the risk of this business model.

In 2013, I began my journey in earnest of relearning marketing. I immersed myself in any kind of professional development opportunities that would satisfy my hunger: networking, memberships, webinars, workshops, mentoring, articles, books. In a way, I am grateful I started when I did. Today, it takes one look at Facebook to see that every man and his dog is advertising their quick path to riches program; so confusing for a new business owner.

About that time, my daughter joined me in the business, fresh from her degree in marketing. We quickly realised this was not a benefit. She had the academic theory, but, like me, had to adapt and learn emerging marketing methods in the real world. Initially we thought it would be a good idea to create a website. This was at the time when websites were more about informing than nurturing and converting. Just putting a website together wasn't the answer.

This time, instead of burn-out, I was suffering from overwhelm, which in turn manifested in a downward spiral of negative thinking. Instead of being inspired, I panicked.

There seemed to be more and more to learn. I couldn't stop digesting information. I was procrastinating. I was experiencing information overload and I felt my head was about to explode. I was trying to rebuild my business at the same time. I spent money on mentors who didn't come through with their promise. I tried the sure-fire strategies for success, but I just wasn't getting anywhere. Meditation helped.

I am not the first, nor will I be the last, person to suffer from burn out. The market place is noisy. There are a lot of people with advice and information about the latest tricks to get leads and sales, but what we also need is wisdom. The kind of wisdom that maintains perspective and helps filter the noise to focus on the right marketing mix; an all-round wisdom that helps maintain life-balance and reduces the likelihood of overload and burnout.

Would things have been different if I had a mentor? I did have a mentor in my government job; the last job before starting my business. The experience helped me in my journey into being my own boss. I was burnt out, mainly because of policy change which adversely impacted on my job role. Whereas previously I had been quite entrepreneurial in my role, changing direction led to a more hands-off approach. That wasn't me and left me depressed and cynical. The mentor program really did help me see an alternative, but I don't think that was the intended outcome.

Intuitive Marketer Principle 15: Find a mentor with the wisdom to guide you to your destination who can filter out unnecessary information, leaving you with the tools for success and room to relax

☐ Determine what your specific goals are
☐ Investigate mentors – choose wisely – check out references

Owning a business can be all consuming. It's transformative and addictive, but if you're not careful, your passion can get trodden on by over-work, over-reaching, and exhaustion. Make time out a priority to recharge your batteries as you go.

CHAPTER 8

THE LIFEBLOOD OF SUCCESS

"A man who views the world the same at fifty as he did at twenty has wasted thirty years of his life." – Muhammad Ali

Intuitive Marketer Principle 16: The wisdom is in the list. Take time to find out who's in your community and why.

Focus

A good way to avoid burnout whilst trying to conquer the myriad of advice and marketing channels, is to start by focusing on the area of marketing that we are good at and to find an alternative or outsource to somebody with good skills in other areas.

For the thirty-something me, in some ways, marketing was a lot simpler. However, I still had to master copywriting, desktop publishing and print media, visual branding and customer service. The success of our programs depended on us anticipating the needs and wants of our target audiences. Targeting and segmenting was our strength and we had processes in place to capture what our customers wanted. We kept our customers by offering more training opportunities, at the same time as acquiring new prospects. We had our lists.

Of all of these, I was good at putting a workshop or conference together; one that flowed with relevant content. This was a technique I learnt from the Head of the Unit. I took over the copywriting of marketing materials because of my ability to get to the point quickly. I adopted the writing style of a Director of the Unit and named it after him. I rarely had any problems getting press releases approved first time by our PR department.

The one skill I didn't have, or so I thought, was public speaking. I shied away from speaking for the first three years in the Unit, but eventually started facilitating breakout sessions within professional development workshops. My first attempt was a disaster; it was a demonstration of the World Wide Web. But I persisted and found that I got good feedback from sessions where I was passionate about the topic at hand. Eventually I designed and led a two-day project management workshop that was delivered on a regular basis across the UK. Since emigrating to Australia, I organised three conferences and regular forums in my government role and was asked to organise one day around e-learning of a two-day regional conference after I left the job. I have presented at state-wide and national workshops and even presented on stage at the Sydney and Melbourne Convention Centres.

I now relish the opportunity to present or facilitate workshops whenever possible. The feedback from my workshops, from hour long to full-day events, has been awesome. My hands-on approach, engaging the room, is designed to activate the room. Sometimes the vibration of the room makes it harder to raise the energy; that's when an interactive approach is most important. It's one thing to deliver a speech from behind a podium as a keynote, but quite another to speak at people in a workshop. Don't you just hate it when people insist on doing that? Workshops should be productive, not extensions of plenary sessions.

How many times has your attention drifted because of a dull presentation that misses the opportunity to impress an audience that could host any number of advocates for the presenter? Instead, you will probably avoid them in the future. I learnt my skills from watching the many presenters and workshop facilitators I have had the fortune to meet over the years.

If you were to ask me today what my favourite marketing skills are, I would say thinking outside the box, copywriting and speaking. All of these give me energy. I have been known to perform, even when sick. But my head has been trying to learn everything. I've been hungry for the latest developments in social media. I've seen countless webinars and videos on social media strategy to attract, nurture and convert prospects. I've attended workshops until my mind has glazed over listening to the same messages again and again. I've heard people who attended numerous workshops by the same presenter in the hope of learning something different. Go figure? With so much information, it's easy to become an addict. A concerned friend recognised this and told me to get out of my head.

There is a balance. We can't stand still. We can't expect to rely solely on the skills we developed ten, twenty or thirty years ago in an ever-evolving society. We must keep learning, but there is a balance.

Wisdom

So much information was in my head that my clients benefited before I did. There is a belief that we should fill our own cup first so that we can flow our abundance to others. How many of us are givers, giving generously even though we don't have the time to put our own advice into action first? Our cup is not yet full. My free advice has helped businesses get on their feet. The paradox is that whilst I have been painstakingly researching to re-position my business, I have given away information to people who have been smart enough to use just one nugget of information to achieve success. I have had to learn that not only is there a monetary value of knowledge, but that it's a valuable asset to assist my business first. Unless we value ourselves, how can we value our work? This is a problem for many business owners who have difficulty in pricing their services. We don't value ourselves.

Having access to, and taking in all this knowledge like a sponge helps to get an overall understanding of the diversity of marketing strategies and tools available but it doesn't mean we must be a master of it all. It's also wise to understand that much of the knowledge you have access to is two dimensional. There's a lot of information about the specifics, but the link to how it fits with other marketing aspects of your business is not explored enough. That's how we lose perspective. For businesses that use social media to get people to workshops as part of their marketing funnel, they look for the easiest way to get them there, but how to present and deliver an excellent all-round customer experience in the physical room is lacking for some and not even on the radar for others.

Not too long ago, people were advising us to grow our database list as fast as possible. Now the emphasis is on the quality of prospects on the list. Earlier I showed that there is much more value to lists. We looked after our database, and our database looked after us; an example of three-dimensional marketing (the breadth of list(s) i.e. segmenting, the length of each list and the added-value of the content of the list (depth). You could also say the **wisdom** is in the list.

Intuitive Marketer Principle 16: The wisdom is in the list.
Take time to find out who's in your community and why.
- ☐ Start a database. Be mindful of spam laws and only incorporate names of people who have elected to receive information.
- ☐ Segment the database.
- ☐ Correspond regularly with your database, but not too regularly.
- ☐ Make your correspondence about them, their needs, wants and interests
- ☐ Consult with your database – don't be afraid to ask for help or feedback
- ☐ Look to your database for expertise

I can present, I can write, I can craft a story. The key to getting out of my head was to focus on my strengths and how to apply them using the tools I had learned. Instead of being in awe of perceived experts, I should have applied their knowledge to my own expertise.

Stop the inertia. Nothing more, nothing less. Figure out what you're good at, apply new knowledge to add value and go for your life. The energy moves from overwhelm, procrastination and fear to excitement motivation and control. This is the lifeblood of success.

CHAPTER 9

RISKY BUSINESS

"We're here to make a dent in the Universe"

- Steve Jobs

Intuitive Marketer Principle 17: Good customer experience comes first, even if you have to take risks to provide it

To get heard in the busy online marketplace of today, it's necessary to stand out from the crowd. For many of us, it's necessary to stand out both online and offline, but we don't always get the balance right.

Unless we are the market leader, we must compete on the continuum from price to quality and make a profit along the way. The conference organiser in me would not understand the rationale for running workshops for free. Our events were a benchmark for competitors to check their fees against. We had a budget template for each conference or workshop and knew our target numbers from breakeven to profit. Even our newsletters were via paid subscription. Run an event for FREE? No way.

To put it simply, our jobs depended on our ability to earn our salaries two years ahead. We weren't familiar with the concept of passive income. We were hungry. Today there are millions to be made with the right online product using an online marketing strategy. People can download what they want to learn or listen or watch online. There's no need to travel, no physical contact with strangers and none of the benefits of networking.

Our success was dependent on being able to deliver quality content and experience in face-to-face environments. Whilst the events appeared to go ahead without any significant glitches, behind the scenes we had some pretty hair-raising moments. Our best conferences and workshops came after traumatic moments behind the scenes. Here are a couple of examples that show that it wasn't always plain sailing when it came to the delivery of our programs.

Imagine you are at a job interview and somebody asks you what you would do in the following scenario:

Outstanding Customer Service

You are organising a week-long study visit to Brussels. Some of the participants, from across the UK, have elected to travel with you as a group via Eurostar from London to Brussels on Monday morning to meet with the rest of the group for dinner at the hotel on Monday evening. The Friday before, you find out that Eurostar trains to Brussels will be on strike on Monday. What do you do?

This question was asked when selecting my successor and it was based on fact.

What complicated things even more was that I was on sick leave with food poisoning from a previous trip to Brussels when I got told we had a dilemma.

If I was an interviewee and asked this question I probably wouldn't have had the creative imagination to get the job (reflecting back to the experience of the younger me with the shade samples). Reality was more interesting.

I went into the office even though I was on sick leave. We checked and discovered that Eurostar trains to Paris were still running and that there was a possibility, but no guarantee that they would stop at Lille in Northern France. That gave us enough to take a risk. We contacted everybody and let them know what was going on. It wouldn't be straight forward for the train travellers. We arranged to meet at a certain time at Waterloo Station in London on Monday morning where we would get our tickets changed to the Paris train, but we would not be seated as a group. A bus was ordered to meet us in Lille. This was on based on a possibility that the train would stop at Lille and that we could all get on the same train.

We tracked everybody but two people who were travelling together. I contacted the office of one and was told she was at a conference and not contactable. This was at a time when most people did not have mobile phones. I then did something extraordinary. I looked up another organisation that might have somebody at the same conference. My hunch was correct. I asked if their attendee was contactable. I then rang this complete stranger and asked a favour to contact the person I was looking for. Amazingly, she was standing right next to the person I was trying to contact. They were good friends. At the end of the study visit I was given a special gift because she was amazed at how I had been able to track her down. There is no way I would have been able to contact her at the weekend as she had not supplied her home address and the office would have been closed. There was also no reason why she would have contacted the office after the conference.

At the railway station people were arriving at different times. There was a queue of people wanting to transfer to the Paris train. I had the tickets from as many of my group members as possible, but it would mean those arriving later would have to queue and wouldn't be seated with the rest of us. Enter Mr Jobsworth. He was sitting behind a ticket booth and had to go into the back office to process the ticket changes on the computer. He took a steady approach and it would take him some time to process the tickets and get back to me just in time for me to give him another batch of tickets to exchange. Needless to say, his deliberate attention to process allowed us to travel together as a group. He will never know how appreciative I was of his excellent customer service that day. We arrived in time for dinner and everybody was excited about the adventure, which set a good tone for the week.

We rarely had speakers who dropped out at the last minute. However, on one occasion our keynote came down with the flu and we had to re-arrange the program. He suggested a replacement who couldn't confirm until 4 pm the day before the conference. We were prepared to take the risk and the replacement was also a good keynote presenter. He was worth the stress and our participants were just as happy listening to him.

Today we talk about people drowning in information. Ironically, we also believed in drowning our event participants in information. Our conference packs were comprehensive. This was in the early days of email and many people did not yet have access. We requested and printed out copies of presentations and workshop materials as well as surveys, information about future workshops and conferences and relevant free publications from the European Commission. Today very little information is provided on the day beyond the program. We can easily download from online or take a photo snapshot of presentation slides. At least a lot of trees will be saved.

As we travelled mostly by public transport to major cities, we would send the participant packages by Red Star Parcels (transported by train). The service was normally very reliable. On one occasion, however, we arrived in London at lunchtime the day prior to a funding conference to find the packages had not arrived. I was with the secretary and a couple of our work-placement team. What did we do? We went on a sightseeing tour, culminating at Harrods. Seriously. Having checked with the university's mail room that the packages had been sent and having cross referenced with the Red Star Parcel office in London, there was not a lot we could do. A good afternoon was had by all and the packages turned up around 6 pm. We took them to the venue and set up before going out to dinner with the speakers. If those packs had not turned up, the conference would have not had crucial information available for participants to read through and take away. It was one of those events announcing new changes to funding. Nobody knew how close they were to not getting the customer experience they were used to,

We stood out because of our customer service. The European Briefing Officer believed in giving everybody as much educational material as possible. It was a value-add to our product offering. As I write this, I realise we already did what the experts are telling us, albeit in a different context. We loaded them up with bonuses.

We created an ambience between the presenters that even led to them coming back many times for repeat performances. We made sure that refreshments and meals were good quality and that there were ample food stations. Don't you just hate it when you have to queue most of the break because there aren't enough serving points? It doesn't do the event any good either when participants are in a bad mood because of it. It's worse than not having food available in the first place.

We stood out because we were consistent. Our visual branding was recognisable. Our event formats were reliable. We attracted expert presenters and workshop facilitators. Our registration processes were systematic. People got pre-event, joining letters confirming the venue, how to get there and other vital information. Today, this kind of consistency is standard practice. The advent of autoresponders and event software makes it easy to automate registration confirmation, reminders, and dispersal of crucial information.

What risks should we be taking today? Many of yesterday's risks have been resolved by today's technology. So, has so much of the fun.

The biggest risk we have today is failure. If we don't get in front of our prospective customer as the expert they are looking for above all others, we risk our business. If we can't sell when the prospect is ready, somebody else will. They win, we lose.

Intuitive Marketer Principle 17: Good customer experience comes first, even if you have to take risks to provide it
- ☐ What are the strengths in your customer service?
- ☐ Where is there room for improvement (relate to your business model)?
- ☐ What measures can you put in place to improve customer service?

Our prospects may be online, but where else do they hang out? It's up to us to reduce the risk by finding our customers in places where others aren't looking, offer and go beyond good service and making sure we offer a memorable customer service experience for the right reasons.

CHAPTER 10

WINNING OFFLINE MARKETING STRATEGIES

"In a crowded marketplace, fitting in is a failure. In a busy marketplace, not standing out is the same is being invisible" – Seth Godin

Intuitive Marketer Principle 18: Face-to-face interaction with customers and prospective customers builds trust, connection, and a sense of belonging that online marketing cannot achieve on its own

Recently I came across a Facebook post in a business group asking members what successful marketing strategies they were using offline. Some of the responses were defensive in that they were justifying why they should be carrying out their marketing online. The responses were simply that as most people hang out online, that's where businesses should be pitching their products and services. This line of response amused me.

The person who asked the question got it right.

Throughout this book I have used examples of offline as well as online marketing strategies and tools. In the first instance, this has been a journey through the development of information technology to simplify marketing for today's businesses. Today's processes are automated and for many it is easy to rely on online marketing to generate significant income. Others are not so lucky and no matter how they try, they haven't cracked the code to success.

There are other marketing channels. These require people to do something different. Over the last few years, my business has been providing marketing services for businesses. Here are three examples of offline marketing strategies that work. There is life beyond online.

Business and Customer Surveys as Engagement Strategies

In two years, we surveyed around 800 business managers for five different community-based training organisations. We actually went and talked to people face-to-face on behalf of the clients. Not only did we get the feedback, some of it negative, yet in each case, the client would start to get enquiries about their services. Surveying people in person is an amazing process in that it engages, or re-engages, the business with the client. The client is telling them, through the survey process, that they are interested in their needs. It works. When the client then adds them to their database to update on services, they already have that connection. Even people who give negative feedback renew their interest. So why are so many people fearful about calling prospects?

We have also surveyed end users face-to-face, in groups and on the phone. The response is very similar to businesses. The action attracts the interest of the customer. In one instance, we found that customers had disconnected from the business because there was no follow-up (business did not send out updates of other products) and the product did not bear any markers that identified the business so people were unable to refer interested parties to the manufacturer. It didn't take much to rectify the problem. It makes good sense to keep in contact with prospects and customers.

Paper-Based Advertising Media

We learnt a valuable lesson three years ago when carrying out a project in a low socio-economic neighbourhood. We had the challenge of surveying a community that had been surveyed to death. We were successful in this part of the research through the inducement of prizes including an iPad. The next stage was to get people to an event that would double-up as a focus group activity afterwards. We put together a humorous flyer that intrigued people enough to come along. When we later spoke to the attendees, we found that they responded to the humour of the flyer. They were intrigued. They also told us that a flyer in the letter box was the best way to get their interest. They told us people in their neighbourhood welcomed junk mail because they could compare supermarket prices for the best deals on food. Flyers are also shared on public community noticeboards. Recently a group of business owners pro-actively posted flyers around town for a first aid course being offered by a client. Paper-based advertising is far from dead. Because it is physical, if it catches the eye and the attention of the right audience, it will stay on the kitchen table longer than on a Facebook page.

Business Networks and Expos

There are a lot of business people competing in low price market segments who want to attract the next level of business customers or new markets. They are competing in a busy marketplace online. I recently advised one such business to check out their local business networks. They are in a market sector that doesn't normally think of business networks as a client attraction point. They went along, built relationships, and got the business they were looking for. Business networks are a good offline marketing strategy because they are social meeting points, build trust and lead to referrals.

The benefits of face-to-face networking happen when you keep turning up. Over time you develop relationships with other business owners. It is about perseverance, especially when you are new and it seems like the network is a closed club. Be selective about networks as it is also possible to get involved in too many.

Expos are also a good marketing strategy. When you think of expos you immediately think of expense, but there are smaller events that businesses can use to test the market. Pick the right expo i.e. the right market and the return on investment far outweighs the investment.

Most of these strategies can be carried out online, but online interaction does not involve the social energy that builds stronger trust and a sense of belonging of human interaction. The growth of referral networks is the social proof.

> **Intuitive Marketer Principle 18: Face-to-face interaction with customers and prospective customers builds trust, connection, and a sense of belonging that online marketing cannot achieve on its own**
> - ☐ What online channels are you currently using to reach, nurture and engage customers and prospective customers?
> - ☐ What offline channels are you currently using to reach, nurture and engage customers and prospective customers?
> - ☐ Where are the opportunities to enhance online engagement with face-to-face and other off-line engagement strategies?

There are many ways to stand out from the competition. But as the online marketplace grows and we are in danger of drowning in the sea of sameness, perhaps more focus on off-line to compliment online strategies could be the saviour of businesses who can fill the gaps online marketing strategies leave open.

CHAPTER 11

PLANNING FOR SUCCESS

*"All you need is the plan, the road map, and the
courage to press on to your destination"*

– Earl Nightingale

**Intuitive Marketer Principle 19: Maintain a focus on planning. As
long as you have a plan, there's no excuse to stop marketing. If
you stop marketing, your business will fail.**

What is a plan? It is an intention and a road map to reach a destination.
How many of us seriously plan? I have been putting together 90-day
plans in my business, but for what purpose?

The thirty-something me didn't really plan how many events we were
going to deliver per year. We just set about organising them during
term breaks (90-day plans by default). Our plan was influenced by the
need for financial security. It was also based on the opportunity to take
a risk and set up new programs alongside those we knew were in
demand. We just planned to be around for the next couple of years.
We were in a market with strong demand. We had a system that
worked. Had we put together a marketing plan, we would have been
a leader in a growth market with a healthy variety of products
including lucrative cash cows to reduce risk. We covered the whole of

the UK, delivering in multiple venues, and had programs that took people to the heart of decision-making (Brussels). We had an effective promotional strategy. We had the four p's of marketing covered (product, place, price, and promotion). This was built on intuition and embedded into practice.

Where our planning did become more deliberate was in the organisation of conferences. Our formula allowed us to deliver a conference on any topic within the European context. We held conferences on rural development, homelessness, adoption and fostering, cyber learning and other diverse topics. In my latter days within the Unit, we attracted participants from thirteen countries to each two-day conference. This is how we did it. We partnered with the experts in the industry. We gave ourselves a twelve to eighteen-month timeline to allow for filtering through the networks. We used our policy and practice formula for the content and planned sufficiently ahead to get the speakers we wanted. It also gave us time to organise exhibitions alongside conference programs. In other words, we engaged in joint ventures. We used other people's lists. We used our brand and credibility (as well as our partners') and we provided opportunities for people to buy other products. Today we could set up a webinar summit.

In contrast, our bread and butter workshops were planned on a 90-day basis. Each school term break would be our time to plot dates, source venues, secure at least the headline presenters or facilitators, and publish the event flyers.

This is not the strategy that I took with me into the business. I just left it to chance and people contacted me with project work. I did once start a plan around services for registered training organisations. I was a qualified quality auditor and had carried out audits for the Victorian Department of Education and Training. I mapped out the services we would offer, but did not follow through. Work was still coming in. I was the coordinator for the national Adult Learners Week campaign in 2011 for Adult Learning Australia. I was a state-wide trainer for impact evaluation in community learning partnerships for three years. I even teamed up with colleagues to audit the National e-Learning Toolboxes. I worked with organisations to secure funding that would engage me as a project manager or to evaluate projects. As a grant writer, I was bringing in sizeable amounts of money for clients and securing work for my business at the same time. This worked as long as funding was available, changes to government policy directions slowed this down considerably.

It was as the brakes went on, that I realised the need to plan and adopt a new strategy. I knew how to write marketing plans. I developed them with clients. I was both technical and also included some innovative thinking when I developed plans for and with others. What I needed was the opportunity to brainstorm with others to guide me with my own marketing plans. This came in the form of a Mastermind group.

The day I got a phone call from another member of a network that I belonged to was a turning point. She wanted to set up a Mastermind group and targeted three people with different perspectives to help her form a small group. She is an incredible woman whose gut instinct never lets her down. On this occasion, three of the four of us would form a group that would last for three years. This group would meet quarterly for a day-long planning session, long enough to work on all three businesses. We shared books and what we'd learned outside of the group, and applied these insights to our business. We left with a plan for the next 90 days and actions to get there. We would then meet by phone every Monday evening for two hours. Woe betide anybody who tried to contact me during this precious time.

I spent these three years relearning marketing. My 90-day plans reflected this learning. I repackaged my products and services and created marketing funnels. The younger versions of me would never have thought of passive income and packaging products and programs as a marketing strategy. We could have done it. There was enough expertise in the European Briefing Unit to produce some brilliant add-on products and services beyond the series of books produced when the Unit was first opened. These were academic in nature and reflected the department, not just the activities of the Unit. I was learning new marketing perspectives, yet I was also becoming aware of strategies that reflected what I already knew; only they were wrapped up in a different language or online software programs that were not yet available to the younger me.

I cannot express how important it is to plan. Write it down. The process of writing down a plan helps with the manifestation process. It doesn't work so well when you type up a plan. Keeping your plan

---

Intuitive Marketer Principle 19: Maintain a focus on planning. As long as you have a plan, there's no excuse to stop marketing. If you stop marketing, your business will fail.

- ☐ Start with a 90-day marketing plan from day one
- ☐ Monitor your plan weekly, monthly and at the end of each 90 days
- ☐ Base your marketing plan on your overall business model and value propositions
- ☐ Build in measurement – cost of acquisition, expected sales and revenue, return on investment (which marketing tools prove the most effective)
- ☐ Include professional development – what marketing skills you will focus on
- ☐ Keep updating your marketing plan every 90 days.

---

in your head, as many business owners say they do, blurs the boundaries, and leads to a moving target and nothing to measure against. Write it down, treat it as your road map and navigate your way through it until you get where you want to go – or change direction.

CHAPTER 12

THE WISDOM OF THE PAST, PRESENT AND FUTURE

"Knowing is not enough. We must apply.
Willing is not enough. We must do." - Johann
Wolfgang von Goethe

Speak to anybody today and they will admit there's a lot of information out there about the latest online marketing tools. Business networking groups abound, particularly in the cities. Entrepreneurs who've hit the jackpot in their businesses (or so we are led to believe) are offering inducements of free workshops. There are also a lot of sharks waiting for the hungry mackerels to gather into their nets, induced by a promise of the magic key to success. As long of the mackerels are hungry enough to pay, the sharks will bait them.

My journey through time in this book has highlighted to me the parallels between offline and online marketing and client engagement. Since the advent of email, the World Wide Web, and Microsoft Office, I have been able to demonstrate that online marketing is constantly evolving in line with innovation in information technology. I was active during the early years of information technology, witnessing and promoting the evolution of many tools we take for granted today.

I have rediscovered the value of offline marketing strategies; how they foster trust and belonging in a magical way that cannot be replicated online. Yet offline strategies can be strengthened by online tools. In the pursuit of wealth, have we got things mixed up? Can customer expectations be fully met online, or do we need offline strategies and tools to bring the human touch to deliver customer service that stands out from the rest?

With internet marketing at saturation point, is offline marketing combined with online the way forward?

Let's take a look at four elements of getting people to buy:

Knowledge of Existence of the Business, its Products and Services

Online: Website, social media, eBay, Online Shop, Google Ads, Facebook marketing

Offline: Business groups, referrals, expos, surveys, radio, television, newspapers, and local newsletters (advertising)

People need to know about your business and what it offers when they need the product or service. The first thing they are likely to do is look online for businesses providing the products or services they want. They are more likely to look at individual websites than online directories or will go to sites such as eBay (where the preference is for the product or service first). Online advertising has now become intuitive and targeted, and people will notice adverts on Google or Facebook relates to something they recently searched for or shown an interest in. The online marketplace is cluttered, so it makes sense to look at offline marketing as well. Join a business network. Start a referral program. Expos are also a good place to promote to those looking for your products or services. What else can you do that doesn't involve the internet?

Trust in the Business and Products/Services

Online: Testimonials (video and written copy), educational content (e-books, webinars, blogs), social media groups (ownership, contribution), relevance (e-newsletters, promoted products and services)

Offline: Face-to-face networking, consistency in customer service, quality standards

As an example, a gardening services business might have a website with testimonials of satisfied customers. They may produce a gardening guide or a monthly gardening blog. They could belong to or own a Facebook group. They could produce a weekly e-newsletter with relevant information for subscribers and will be promoting products and services for the current or upcoming season. They could have a loyalty program for customers, who benefit from the consistently good customer experience (they become the online testimonials).

The business belongs to a local business network and gets referrals. Other businesses (e.g. cleaning) may also comply with quality standards and will promote this on all marketing materials both online and offline.

Despite the plethora of tools available to develop trust online, nothing compares to face-to-face. Face-to-face interaction could make the difference between email and junk mail, and foster long term support for your business.

Need for Your Products or Services

Online: Stop images and videos, blogs, educational content (e-guides, articles, webinars), web copy (focused on problem and solution), guarantees, testimonials, competitions.

Offline: newspapers, trade magazines, radio, events, demonstrations (markets)

People respond to images that invoke emotion. Whether it is online images or in brochures or flyers, images that relate to surprise, intrigue or shock will get a second glance. Web copy must also focus on enhancing the problem and what happens if you don't solve it; then followed by why the site owner is the ONLY solution. Back these up with testimonials and no risk guarantees to convince the visitor. This is dependent on the visitor landing on your website or finding your promotional ad with image on another website or video site.

To enhance local reach, replicate the problems and solutions focus with images in local media. How often have you been at a market, seen a demo of a cool, labour saving, kitchen appliance and just had to buy it? You hadn't previously imagined you needed it, but seeing what it could do in real time (no hidden trickery) made it so hard to resist.

Saving Time

Online: Webinars, online ordering, search engines

Offline: Retail shops

Webinars save time. They reduce the need to attend meetings, workshops and training sessions face-to-face. No travel time involved. Search online, find something you want and order it straight away. No need to go to the shopping centre. On the other hand, shopping centres are good for retail therapy – customers can see, feel, try on and smell before they buy. They can also buy a variety of items and enjoy the experience of spending money. We buy online because we think we need things fast, but in doing so, we forget the experience of using our senses and the satisfaction of making an informed choice – a choice of the mind, heart, and gut. Maybe retailers should start promoting the ability to touch, feel and try out as unique selling features over buying online.

Saving Money

Online: eBay, online shops, sales, payment gateways

Offline: Coupons/vouchers, loyalty cards.

Buying online cuts out the middle man and can be cheaper than buying from a shop. Payment can be made immediately and can be reversed if the goods are not received. Coupons and vouchers are still used by price conscious buyers. Supermarkets produce weekly offers catalogues and target people who look for, and compare, offers of the week. Retailers use loyalty cards that offer points that can be surrendered for products, services, or cash.

With imagination, businesses can enhance their sales and profitability by combining both online and offline marketing. Businesses that rely on online marketing are promoting their products and services in an increasingly crowded marketplace. Many of the successful online marketers use client attraction, nurturing and conversion strategies, sometimes including face-to-face interactions. These interactions could be improved by enhancing the customer experience that will lead to higher conversions. There are bricks and mortar businesses that have a fear of online marketing based on their lack of knowledge and skills, but they do possess excellent customer service skills that they do not immediately appreciate. Their fear or lack of knowledge of the benefits of the online environment could be reduced with a greater understanding how digital marketing can enhance what they are already doing right and can fill in some gaps in the process of nurturing customers and getting repeat business. It's easy to find out who they are. Look for the businesses who use email addresses ending in Hotmail, Gmail, or the name of their local telecommunications provider.

Businesses that traditionally sell one product at a time could learn to use their customer database to offer additional products to enhance the pleasure of the first purchase, or they could engage their customers through offering benefits for referrals. They could use the customer database to survey them as an excuse to stay in touch. They could invite them to special events. It is at least seven times easier to get repeat business from existing customers than to find new ones. Whilst some businesses are better at offline customer engagement, they could be leaving money on the table by not using online tools available to them.

Information technology will continue to progress and the wise business person will keep an eye on developments. As the online environment becomes even more crowded, shrewdness business owners will again re-discover the value of combining online and offline marketing strategies. Future success may depend on this.

CHAPTER 13

THE MONEY GAME

*"If you don't value your time, neither will others.
Stop giving away your time and talents. Value
what you know & start charging for it."*

- Kim Garst

Intuitive Marketer Principle 20: Play the money game. Avoid charging per hour in favour of a fixed fee, incorporate a passive-income source and create a product/service funnel to maximise income.

With respect to money, many service-based business owners, not just start-ups, have difficulty in pricing their programs. Here are three challenges – pricing per hour, results/fixed price, packaging, and funnel pricing.

Charging per Hour

*"You don't get paid for the hour. You get paid for
the value you bring to the hour" – Jim Rohn*

In some industries, charging per hour is a good benchmark to start pricing services. There are formulas on the internet to work out how much to charge per hour. In the absence of these formulas, a respected consultant once told me to decide what I wanted to earn and multiply by three (to cover overheads etc.). The final price depends on what the market will stand and what the competition is charging. A person who charges at the higher end of the scale is either working with contracts that expect these prices or has obtained a positive perception about the quality of their services. There are consultants who should be charging for quality, but find themselves charging at the bottom end of the scale. They could argue to themselves that this is what the market expects, but a greater influence is mind-set. They don't believe they are that good and don't deserve to charge at the higher end.

I started at a rate per hour which I have since increased after being told that my rates were low (my services were costed into funding applications). At the same time, clients I worked with wanted services as cheaply as possible because they were thinking of me as an extension of their staff. Today a notional rate per hour is used internally in my business costings only and is used as a benchmark. Even my assistant's time is charged out on service, not rate per hour. My recent journey into updating my marketing skills led me to changing my price per hour model to a results-based, fixed price model which made more sense to my self-worth.

Results/Fixed Price

I recently reviewed the marketing strategy of a cleaning company. Business was going well. Too well. They were so busy they didn't have the staff to cover for occasional sickness; so busy because they were charging bottom dollar per hour. They were also attracting the kind of customers who measured work by the hour. If they didn't spend all the contracted hours cleaning, then customers complained. The business owner argued that by targeting larger clients, they could charge more and be respected for the quality of their work irrespective of the time it takes. We reviewed what the competition was charging and confirmed they were charging at the bottom end of the price scale. The problem with charging on lowest price is that these businesses go bankrupt. We did, however, also identify that some competitors were competing on fixed price; a strategy that could help our client attract larger clients who were more interested in quality and consistency than watching the clock.

Fixed cost pricing focuses on what the customer wants – achievement of results. Business owners that invest in the packages offered by the marketing gurus don't work out the number of hours involved first; they are drawn to the offer by a customer-focused articulation of the results and benefits offered if they follow this or that strategy or framework. It's about return on investment; mainly the impact on sales and profits. Only after the results and benefits come the features in importance to the customer. Fixed cost pricing also allows the business owner to move away from pricing per hour mind-set. Align the results and benefits to testimonials and examples and the prospect has little concern for price per hour. They just want a piece of the success pie.

Sometimes it's difficult to get away from pricing per hour, especially when this is required for some government grants and tenders, but it makes more sense to charge for the service based on benefits and results.

Packaging

When quoting on fixed price, another feature, that is commonly used today is that of packaging bonuses to create a sense of value-add. Information technology has made it easier to offer additional online software and training programs for free as inducements to take up the main offer. Twenty years ago, businesses might have been able to offer books and training manuals, but there would have been costs of production and distribution involved. Today these are available for online download. The prospect gets additional benefits (for free). We are being told by the marketing experts to offer three additional benefits, such as online programs and free attendance at workshops. The free attendance at workshops is part of the journey to the high end offers and as previously indicated, is a good way to garner trust, a necessary component for building a loyal repeat customer base.

Funnel Pricing

Even though we were prolific in the number of workshops and conferences we delivered, we did not strategically organise workshops with a view to upgrading to the next level. Even our postgraduate program for European Liaison Officers didn't have a direct pathway into it. Most of our workshops were at the same level; different disciplines, but at the same level. Today it's about having the ability to offer more services or products as a customer retention strategy. Maybe we could retain our pricing policy today for our mainstream workshops but pay more attention to the pathways into and from the programs.

There has been a marked shift in pricing of training workshops over the last few years; shift based on purpose. In the 1990s, I would cost our programs based on break even and anticipated audience numbers. Participants would pay for the information and education they receive from the event. Today, entrepreneurs charge under 100 dollars, if at all, to attract people and then educate them just enough to then sell their high-end programs. For somebody like me, this means adopting a completely new mind-set and program offerings. Whereas in the past the workshop would be all that was offered, now my focus has moved to delivering workshops at a low price that lead to further services and even products.

I used to present at conferences and never considered selling from the stage. Today I play it by ear depending on what the conference is about as to whether to offer a follow-up product or service at the end of my presentation, but where possible I request a trade table or opportunities to leave promotional materials.

This new approach has meant that I have had to review my services. Over the past three years I have developed online programs and resources that can be sold as stand-alone passive income as well as part of a marketing funnel. I have an ultimate grant writing program complete with all the checklists and templates as well as manuals and audio modules needed to write successful grant applications both large and small. My funnel also includes introductory guides for free,

free webinars (that are also recorded), training workshops and a mentoring program for grant writers. I have replicated this model for my other services. This approach allows businesses to nurture prospects firstly into their programs and then into higher end offers. A business can start with a free consult or offer, leading to a below $100 offer, a $300-$500 offer, through to $5,000 and above. In each case, experts suggest that we round down to the $7 below our price point (e.g. $97).

Whatever pricing strategy or strategies we adopt, they are of no benefit if we can't measure the cost of sale. How much we spend on social media for example, must be lower than the price we charge unless we are deliberately looking for customers before profits. Promotions through face-to-face networks or promotional flyers also incur costs. Budgeting and the cost per sale can get complicated through the funnel process. Experts show this process, but they don't appear to factor in the time it takes to develop and run a live webinar for example. Developing programs and e-books takes time but appears to be forgotten about in the budget process. The money game has certainly changed.

Fundamentally, though, we must value our time. If we don't, then why should anybody else?

> **Intuitive Marketer Principle 20: Play the money game. Avoid charging per hour in favour of a fixed fee, incorporate a passive-income source and create a product/service funnel to maximise income.**
>
> ☐ Plan at least three income generation streams to minimise impact of sudden changes in any one stream (e.g. services, products, investments)
>
> ☐ Always start with results that the customers are looking for. Use these to re-enforce the value of your product or service.
>
> ☐ (Internally) cost your time based on available days and percentage of your time actually on the job. At least 50% of your available time may be spent on overhead activities such as marketing, administration and planning. Build in costs to keep the business operating (e.g. vehicles, accounting, utilities, rent). $40 per hour as an employee may become $200 per hour of direct time on activities to generate your desired annual income. There are online calculators to help you determine your fee per hour (such as http://www.flyingsolo.com.au/hourly-rate-calculator for solopreneurs).
>
> ☐ Use the rate per hour to inform a fixed fee proposal relating to achievement of results.
>
> ☐ Set up a funnel of products and services to generate repeat custom

CHAPTER 14

A MARKETING STRATEGY FOR A START-UP

If I were to start my business today, here are 11 things I would put in place:

- o Make marketing a priority. Start with a plan from day one.
  To start in business without a marketing plan is a guarantee for failure irrespective of what the business is selling – product or service. Even a business with ready-made customers must cast a wider net.

- o Develop my products and services and funnel them into target markets
  To stand out from competitors involves the ability to use the creative brain to gain trust, nurture the prospect and get them to repeat buy. Create free collateral, basic offers and pathways into higher end sales.

- o Plan to create products that will produce a passive income stream
  A business that relies on contract work or working directly with a client is akin to buying a job. Avoid risks in the event of sickness or other issues. Create a passive stream of steady

income.

o Research competitors – find out what they're doing and gaps in their marketing
Avoid competing in a sea of sameness. Be creative. Find and exploit a gap in the way competitors are marketing their products and services.

o Identify my business's unique selling proposition and use it
Why should customers buy from my business above others? Have the confidence to use our credentials, expertise and what sets us apart.

o Purchase a web domain with a relevant name and email accounts
People research the internet before making buying decisions. A website is crucial to being in the game. Associated with a website are email addresses. A business with an email address aligned to their website or business name appears more professional than one aligned to a generic email host.

o Build a website that talks to my target audience, is results focused and makes it as easy as possible for visitors to take the next step (e.g. download e-guide, free manual, buy a product, make an appointment or phone)
Websites must have a purpose, whether to sell, nurture prospects or provide information. They must be able to keep a visitor's attention beyond eight seconds. People visit websites to solve problems. We should oblige.

o Put together a marketing skills acquisition plan with priorities and targets
It's far better to plan for updating and keeping abreast of new marketing tools and practices than to have to play catch up later-on.

o Invest in an autoresponder/email marketing system (good for newsletters, landing pages, database lists) and use it
A customer relationship management (CRM) database

system is crucial to acquire and nurture new customers. An autoresponder system also provides opportunities to acquire and communicate with prospects and clients. Larger businesses may invest in more powerful online marketing automation systems.

o   Focus on social media that relates to my products and services
Social media is a good way to point people to the website, but also involves good platforms for talking to prospects. It would be foolhardy not to consider Facebook's mega marketing machine or YouTube's video search engine capability.

o   Join relevant networks – online and offline. Avoid networks with competitors / look for networks that include the target audience.
People don't just hang out online. Networking builds credibility, authority, liking and trust. Persevere.

I would effectively develop a business model that would focus on the needs of my market niche by developing a value proposition through my products and services. These products and services would evolve with my market by using my creative brain to stand out from the competition. I would use online and offline marketing channels to deliver an enjoyable customer experience. At the same time, I would make a concerted effort to keep abreast of new marketing techniques and opportunities.

CHAPTER 15

AN INTUITIVE FUTURE

"The best way to predict the future is to create it"
– Peter Drucker

As I write this chapter, my brain is full. I have reached saturation point with my journey through the leaps and bounds of changes to online marketing over the last few years. My journey through this book has involved some interesting threads. One of these is the evolution of information technology and its application to marketing. From learning binary code in school, through to the influence of Microsoft Office, the World Wide Web, the Information Society, and today's online marketing tools, it seems, I already understood the fundamentals of digital technology. What we have today is a proliferation of tools. Online marketing is upgrading the analogue strategies of yesterday into the digital age. It is making it easier for businesses to satisfy the needs and wants of today's consumers by solving a problem or satisfying desire and making it as easy as possible to buy once the decision to purchase is made.

Today, we are living with online social networks. The younger versions of me enjoyed the thrill of working with people and networks as technology was not as advanced as it is today. Here I am, a real-life passenger of the development of marketing tools and information technology over the last few decades. The fax machine gathering dust, annual visits to Olympia, the satellite demo that nearly ended in disaster. The ride has been amazing.

My marketing journey started as a clueless bystander in a simpler age yet with the same principles we apply today. From emotional response marketing, to database marketing, focusing on customer experience, networking, and face-to-face contact, there is still a place for non-IT related marketing activity. This journey hasn't been about the academic principles of marketing (although I could talk about them if I wanted). This journey has been about the normal day-to-day contact a grass-roots business would experience with the world of marketing.

Even with the proliferation of marketing tools and strategies, face-to-face contact is imperative. On the one hand, successful marketing gurus build face-to-face activities into their marketing funnels and those of their clients. People do respond more favourably when they have witnessed the prospective seller in action. I prioritise what emails I read based on whether I've seen the author in action. On the other hand, I have seen first-hand, how people re-engage with suppliers of products and services when they've been personally interviewed. In this age of online technology, it is still important to reach out with physical contact. Robot technology has not yet taken over. We are still human after all.

The visionaries and founding fathers of the Information Age were spot on over thirty years ago. The Information Age has allowed us to work from home because of the internet, enabling us to trade and learn new knowledge and skills. We are a connected global community. I wonder what they would say today looking forward to the next thirty years?

I stand today at the crossroads with tomorrow, harnessing the wisdom of the past with a mission to continue the digital journey more confident of its place in, and how it compliments, the physical world of marketing.

Whatever happens in the future, providing there isn't a world-wide technological catastrophe, what we do will become even more intrinsically integrated with evolving information technology. We can't avoid that. I can't help thinking that the overall winners will be those who also value and apply the power of offline interaction with our target clients. How can we take customer service to the next level? As Dr Seuss said, "only you can control your future".

Stay informed. Stay wise.

Here's to the future.

BONUS CHAPTER

THE MARKETING MATRIX

Starting with Vision, Goals, and Purpose, use this marketing matrix alongside the Intuitive Marketer Principles in this book. Make sure you cover all boxes to create a balanced marketing model that benefits you and your business.

PERSONAL ATTRIBUTES	BUSINESS/MARKETING MODEL	BRAND
SELF-EDUCATION	VISION, GOALS and PURPOSE	CREATIVITY
TIME MANAGEMENT	RESOURCES	MARKETING CHANNELS

Vision, Goals and Purpose

If you don't have a vision for your business, your plans will have neither clear purpose nor destination. Regularly update your plans (refer to chapter 11).

- ☐ Develop a clear Vision
- ☐ Determine your organisation's Purpose
- ☐ Define up to five measurable business Goals (in line with your Purpose to help you achieve your Vision)
- ☐ Use these to inform your plans

Business/Marketing Model

Make sure you are pitching the right products or services to the right target market, that can pay, and that the market needs and wants (also refer to Chapter 1).
- ☐ Set up your business/marketing model:
  - o Target market(s)
  - o Products and services
  - o Value Proposition
  - o Customer attraction, nurture and retention strategies
  - o Product/service delivery channels
  - o Resource requirements
  - o Stakeholders and partners
- ☐ Evaluate the model for financial viability:
  - o Cost of producing products or services (break down into tasks)
  - o Cost of attraction, nurturing and retention strategies
  - o Cost of delivery of products and services
  - o Ability of target market(s) to pay
  - o Annual budget based on most likely case scenarios
- ☐ Risk Management:
  - o Identify potential risks
  - o Determine likelihood of risks occurring and impacts
  - o Adjust model to mitigate risks

Brand

Targeting is a two-way street. Buyers also target suppliers based on their perception of the brand. The more successful the brand, the more successful the business. Build your brand to help your target market differentiate you from the competition and choose you (also refer to chapter 3).
- ☐ Determine the Values of your business/operation
- ☐ Determine your unique selling proposition (USP)/point of difference
- ☐ Operationalise your Business Model according to your Values and USP
- ☐ Create visual branding templates
- ☐ Embed brand related activities into your policies and procedures

Creativity

Discounting on price? The first to the bottom goes out of business strategy? So, why do it? Break through with a creative mind-set. Use it to solve problems and develop new products and services (see chapter 4).

- ☐ Use every opportunity to use your creative streak (everybody has one)
- ☐ Look for creative solutions to challenges
- ☐ When you can't compete on price, get creative

Marketing Channels

Market, market, market from day one. Minimise pressure to invest in the latest online marketing system by planning your marketing channel requirements, incorporating both online and offline alternatives. At the same time, key up-to-date with media tools and programs and consider being an early adopter to get ahead of the competition (see chapters 10 and 12).

- ☐ Invest in online marketing channels
  - o Website
  - o Social media
  - o Webinars
  - o Marketing automation system
  - o CRM database
  - o Video
  - o Podcasts
  - o Directories
  - o Google
  - o Newsletters
- ☐ Invest in offline marketing channels
  - o Networks
  - o Promotional leaflets and materials
  - o Business cards
  - o Expo's
  - o Media
  - o Sponsorship
  - o Directories
  - o Phone

- Publications
- Workshops
- Visits

Resources
Avoid burnout. Invest in resources to increase productivity, save time, and increase profits. Delegating to staff or outsourcing could save you time that you could spend on income generation activities. Partner with others to reach new markets. Use technology and software for cost effective marketing (see chapters 5 and 7).
- ☐ Staff
- ☐ Virtual assistants
- ☐ Outsourcing expertise
- ☐ IT equipment
- ☐ Recording devices
- ☐ Software (one-off and subscription)
- ☐ Joint venture partners

Time Management
A risk to business owners is that the business takes over your time. Over-work leads to reduced productively and can lead to burnout (refer to chapter 7).
- ☐ Set boundaries – work-time, family-time, me-time
- ☐ Plan and take regular vacation breaks – diarise
- ☐ Take regular breaks during the day
- ☐ Outsource tasks to leave time so you can focus on income generating activities

Self-Education
Most business owners go into business because of their technical skills and passion, and don't have the marketing skills. Intuition will play a role, yet there is a lot of opportunity to develop marketing skills both online and offline (for more detail, refer to chapter 2).
- ☐ Set up a plan for professional development:
  - Networks
  - Online programs
  - Workshops
  - Books

- o Mastermind group
- o Mentor

Personal Attributes

Today's marketing is about focusing on providing a solution for the buyer, making it easier for them to purchase from you. In a crowded marketplace, businesses must be able to stand out and take risks (see chapter 9).

- ☐ Success mind set
- ☐ Risk taker
- ☐ Willing to fail fast (and bounce back)
- ☐ Think-outside-the-box
- ☐ Creative

SUMMARY

INTUITIVE MARKETING PRINCIPLES

1: Build in marketing from day one. Aim for at least 20% of your available time to be engaged in marketing activities.

2: Ensure your business model is sustainable. If not, change it immediately.

3: Use the tools of the day to evoke emotion. People respond to words, expressions and imagery.

4: Education is key to demonstrating trust and credibility. Teach them something they don't know and you are positioning yourself as an expert.

5: Strive to keep up to date with your marketing knowledge. Use a variety of channels which may include: books, workshops, webinars, Mastermind groups, networks, mentors and literature.

6: To be the market leader in your niche, surround yourself with the right experts and networks. Be prepared to take risks.

7: Know your niche and be consistent.

8: Be creative. Do something different. If it works, let it become your signature trademark.

SUMMARY

9: Be different, be visible, be unique. Use your creative brain.

10: Changes in technology move fast. Harness technology as an innovator and keep an eye out for new developments.

11: Harness the power of technology to stay ahead of your competition.

12: Keep your focus on the problem you are solving for the client in front of you, right up to the point of delivery and beyond.

13: In the digital age, the currency of genuine trust should incorporate old world offline strategies.

14: Build in time out. It does not have a negative impact on your productivity.

15: Find a mentor with the wisdom to guide you to your destination who can filter out unnecessary information, leaving you with the tools for success and room to relax.

16: The wisdom is in the list. Take time to find out who's in your community and why.

17: Good customer experience comes first, even if you have to take risks to provide it.

18: Face-to-face interaction with customers and prospective customers builds trust, connection, and a sense of belonging that online marketing cannot achieve on its own.

19: Maintain a focus on planning. As long as you have a plan, there's no excuse to stop marketing. If you stop marketing, your business will fail.

20: Play the money game. Avoid charging per hour in favour of a fixed fee, incorporate a passive-income source and create a product/service funnel to maximise income.

EPILOGUE

Congratulations on reading to the end of this book. I trust you have picked up some valuable concepts and checklists along the way, that you can use in your business. I put this book together with the small business owner in mind, who is struggling to make sense of everyday marketing principles, When I realised I needed to do something or go broke, I got lost in the overwhelming amount of advice about the best way to attract clients, build and promote marketing funnels to get and retain customers. The key word is funnels; how to take the client from free to high end offers through a sequence of online techniques. There wasn't a lot of focus on mixed marketing channels - strategically using a range of marketing tools, offline as well as online, according to customer segments and their habits. There didn't appear to be a balance; it seemed to be all online or nothing in some cases. If I got lost trying to navigate all this information, then others would too.

Ironically, I once worked for a market leader in its niche and have experienced success. Thus, I set out to take you, the reader, through my journey from rise to fall and rise again, that encourages you to respect what you already intuitively know about marketing, and to introduce you to some tools and concepts that will give you some breathing space to think about planning your marketing, before you get carried away by the 'experts'. Depending on where you are in your marketing journey, some will be more relevant than others, at the moment.

This is a unique journey for each, and every business owner who reads this book. One message may be more relevant to you than another that may be more relevant to others. The technology goal posts keep changing; this is a given. What works well today will be an 'old-fashioned' memory tomorrow. Yet the principles are timeless. I'd love

EPILOGUE

to hear how you get on and what has made most impact for you.

Have a great ride and don't forget to start taking marketing seriously now, if you haven't done so already.

ABOUT THE AUTHOR

Emigrating to Australia in 2000, Pat Grosse feels like she's been living two lifetimes in one. So much so, that when she fulfilled her dream of starting a business, she buried her marketing experience and made the number one mistake of not marketing from day one. Like many business owners, she initially relied on her reputation with an influx of work that supported her business comfortably through the first three years.

Pat has an entrepreneurial spirit that has sustained her in two long term jobs that allowed her to be creative and self-directing, attributes that helped her through the transformation of her business model. It wasn't a fast transition, taking another three years to update her skills and create new programs and services. Pat now has two business models – one that supports not-for-profit organisations to achieve their dreams (including millions of dollars in grant funding) and one that applies her marketing wisdom and background understanding of information technology to help transform businesses.

She has a Degree in Business Administration with a focus on marketing and a post-graduate entry Diploma in Professional Studies in Education Marketing. She also has a handful of Diplomas covering a range of business disciplines. Despite this, much of what she has experienced and written about in this book, is not covered in academic learning. Small business owners have different experiences to corporations; more hands-on and personal. For this reason, the best people to learn from are business owners who've experienced the highs and lows of success. In Pat's case, as an early adopter, she's also been involved in using and promoting information technology that we take for granted today, and will continue to embrace new marketing

ABOUT THE AUTHOR

tools alongside tried and tested methods.

Pat has written a number of articles on topics such as marketing, grant writing and business partnerships. She has also written grant writing and project management training packages, as well as a business partnerships toolbox.

Pat can be found on:

www.springboardtrainingsolutions.net

www.thecommunityentrepreneur.com

www.partnershipstoolbox.com

Are you:
- a business start-up, keen to get your marketing working for you right from the start?
- a business wanting to expand your current marketing channels to attract more customers?
- ready to increase your customer base and sales with a marketing game plan for your business?

MARKETING GAME PLAN

We know how important it is to have a marketing plan and how overwhelming it is to learn what you need to know as quickly as possible to assist with making the right decisions. Our Marketing Game Plan services will guide you in putting together a plan that will help you:

- Set your marketing strategy against your Vision, Purpose, Goals and Values – it's YOUR plan
- Test your Business Model to make sure it is viable – you're on the right path
- Identify and use your Brand Values to set you apart from others – you stand out for the right reasons
- Focus on the right market(s) with the right marketing messages – gain credibility
- Sort out which online and offline marketing strategies are most relevant for you right now - focus on the right strategies for your business
- Engage with on-the-ground learning opportunities - to build your marketing expertise and networks
- Use your available resources in the most cost-effective way - maximise profits with the least effort.

For information about our marketing services, go to www.springboardtrainingsolutions.net or email us on findus@springboardtrainingsolutions.net with subject line "Intuitive marketer - Marketing Game Plan."

<u>NOTES</u>

NOTES

www.ingramcontent.com/pod-product-compliance
Lightning Source LLC
Chambersburg PA
CBHW070735220326
41598CB00024BA/3431